WHARF

*'Beautiful Wharfedale, so sweet and so fair,
Nowhere in England can with thee compare.'*

From a song written by Willie Foster of Beckermonds
and traditionally sung at the George Inn,
Hubberholme, at New Year.

WHARFEDALE

A David Leather

Smith
Settle

First published in 1991 by
Smith Settle Ltd
Ilkley Road
Otley
West Yorkshire
LS21 3JP

ISBN 1 870071 70 0

Designed, printed, and bound by
SMITH SETTLE
Ilkley Road, Otley, West Yorkshire LS21 3JP

CONTENTS

For Midge, who walked them all

INTRODUCTION

Here is a new kind of guide for walkers in Wharfedale. In four introductory chapters, there is an explanation of the landscape of the area, the history of the dale, its villages and folklore, the birds and animals likely to be encountered, and some of the flowers and plants, all with specific reference to Wharfedale. Twenty beautiful walks, ranging from three and a half to fourteen miles, contain descriptions of outstanding points of interest likely to be seen along the way. Some of the walks concentrate, for example, on geology or birds, though most combine a variety of subjects. Directions are kept to a minimum and are complemented by clear maps.

The initial idea for this original series was hatched at Smith Settle, the publishers, and I was asked if I would tackle this first book, together with a similar volume on Wensleydale. Not only did it involve walking hundreds of miles, reading the literature on the history of Wharfedale, making notes and taking photographs, but it was work that also needed help from specialist local experts. Members of the Wharfedale Naturalists Society and others answered my many questions and provided up-to-date records regarding the wildlife in the dale.

Jeremy Taylor has done a great job on the beautifully executed line drawings, and Janet Rawlins has provided some of her stunning watercolours of wild flowers. The excellent photographs are by Trevor Croucher, and the author.

Where paths are easy to follow, directions are minimal and tend to be at the beginning of each paragraph. More detailed directions are given where there is a likelihood of missing the way. The route and adjacent features are shown on a large map for each of the walks, and should be sufficient to find the way. However, you may like to make use of the appropriate Ordnance Survey 1:25,000 Outdoor Leisure map (2½ inches to the mile) to identify distant views. The smaller scale Landranger maps at 1:50,000 are also useful in relating the walk to the surrounding countryside. In using the grid references given at the start of each walk, don't forget to read along the foot (or top) of the map first.

This is a personal selection of walks which are by no means official routes, and although great care has been taken to follow rights of way, these often change in small ways. Additions and modifications are made from time to time, often to the benefit of walkers. Where a section of the route departs from the right of way, mention is made of it.

All the walks are circular, and suitable parking places at the beginning of each walk are indicated. Details of the available public transport are also given. The time given for each walk does not allow for stops, picnics or photography, so if you are out for the day, add about a third to the stated walking time. Any strenuous climbs or exposed routes are detailed at the beginning of each walk, but a good pair of walking boots and waterproofs are always advisable.

The description of each walk draws attention to all kinds of things to look out for and find along the way, but there are plenty left to discover for yourself. It requires some concentration to train oneself to see and hear signs of wildlife, and to develop a 'seeing eye' in an appreciation of what lies behind the scenery and what the landscape can reveal. I find, for instance, that while I am admiring some newly-found flower I don't hear the bird which is singing above me, or when looking at the geology I forget the wild flowers. It takes practice, since anyone can look at the countryside but few can *see* what is there.

When you are out in the Dales, take back with you happy memories, notes, sketches or photographs, but please leave undisturbed the wild flowers, rocks and fossils for the enjoyment of others. Remember to follow the Country Code, and respect the life and work of the countryside.

I would like to thank John Ward, Michael Chadwick and Sunniva Green who gave me help with the bird chapter, Joan Duncan and Audrey Gramshaw who checked the flowers, and Freda Draper who advised on insects. Thanks too to Dr David Turner who gave advice on the geology of the upper dale, and Dinie Blake on the history of Wharfedale. I would like particularly to thank Mark Whitley of Smith Settle who has given so much advice and encouragement in the production of this book.

A D Leather
Ilkley 1991

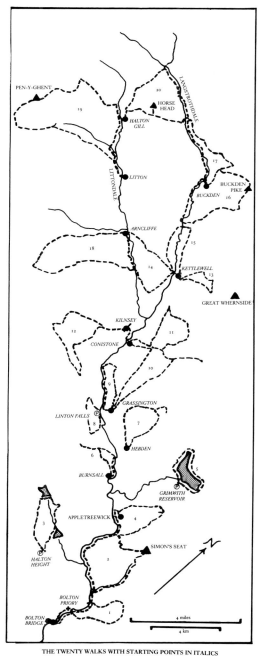

THE TWENTY WALKS WITH STARTING POINTS IN ITALICS

ix

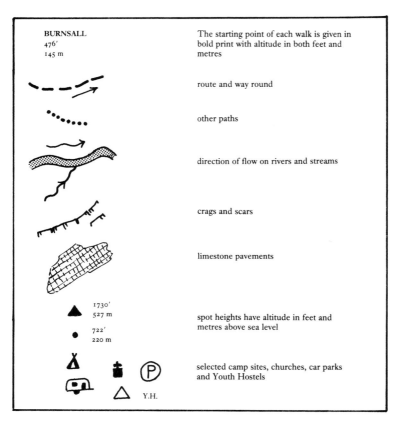

BURNSALL
476'
145 m

The starting point of each walk is given in bold print with altitude in both feet and metres

route and way round

other paths

direction of flow on rivers and streams

crags and scars

limestone pavements

1730'
527 m

722'
220 m

spot heights have altitude in feet and metres above sea level

Y.H.

selected camp sites, churches, car parks and Youth Hostels

KEY TO MAPS

PUBLIC TRANSPORT

British Rail operate to Ilkley and Skipton, from where there are bus services into Wharfedale, though from Ilkley it is only a summer service.

Keighley and District Travel run the bus service in Wharfedale between Skipton and Buckden via Grassington, and from Ilkley via Bolton Abbey and Burnsall to Grassington. Care is needed when planning, as times vary on different days of the week and between summer and winter. An excellent and comprehensive timetable entitled *Dales Connections* gives all these bus services with rail connections. It is free from Keighley and District Travel Ltd, 6 Central Buildings, Keighley Road, Skipton BD29 2NS (0756 795331). The latest editions should be available from the Tourist Information Centre at Skipton (0756 792748) and the National Park Centre at Grassington (0756 752748).

ROCKS AND THE LANDSCAPE

Wharfedale has a beauty and charm of its own and has been called 'The Queen of the Dales'. You may have memories, perhaps, of times spent visiting Bolton Abbey, picnicking at Burnsall or paddling in the river above Yockenthwaite. The late Walter Flesher, broadcaster and naturalist, always maintained that the River Wharfe was the most beautiful river in England, and who would disagree? The Wharfe is a gem among rivers, as it rushes between crags and scars, plunges through narrow clefts and winds peacefully through meadows and woodland. Its valley – together with that of Littondale – is a landscape with a special beauty and character of its own, from Beckermonds and Foxup to Bolton Bridge. This is the twenty-three mile (37km) stretch of the dale covered by the walks in this book, and which lies just within the Yorkshire Dales National Park. Through the dale from one end to the other runs the Dales Way, the beautiful seventy-three mile (117km) long-distance footpath from Ilkley to Bowness-on-Windermere, founded in 1970 by Colin Speakman.

The present-day scenery of this delightful dale is the result of a blend of the natural landscape and the influence man has had on his surroundings; a blend on the one hand of the nature of the rocks, the effect of ice and water and the mantle of soils and plants, and on the other hand of the human touches which have been added mainly over the last few hundred years, of winding roads, quarries and mines, drystone walls, field barns and the picturesque villages which make Wharfedale so distinctive.

The rocks are the backbone of the landscape. The limestones and grits appear at the surface in spectacular fashion at Kilnsey Crag (*walk 12*) and Simon's Seat (*walk 2*), at Parson's Pulpit and Conistone Pie (*walk 11*), and in continuous scars along the valley sides and in the river bed itself. The geology of Wharfedale is very simple. The rocks are all sediments which were once laid down in water as sand or mud. They are all of the Carboniferous Age and so formed in ancient seas, lagoons and deltas 350 to 325 million years ago. Since that time the sands and muds have been compressed, compacted and cemented into solid limestones, sandstones, and softer mudstones and shales.

The Craven Fault   Wharfedale has been sliced across the middle by an ancient fracture known as the Craven Fault which runs roughly west-east, south of Grassington but north of Burnsall. Along the line of the fault there is a striking change in the rock type, from mainly limestones to the north of the fault to the thick layers of shales to the south. You can see the result of the fault today where the River Wharfe drops several feet over the limestone at Linton Falls (*walk 8*), and between Skirethorns and Bordley (*walk 12*) where there is a great contrast in vegetation from one side of the fault to the other. Lying near the fault on its southern side near Burnsall and Thorpe is a line of green hills of pure limestone known as reef knolls (*walk 6*).

The Limestone Country North of the Craven Fault   Two types of limestone are to be seen in Wharfedale. First a solid slab 600 feet (180m) thick, known as the Great Scar limestone, which is beautifully exhibited in the cliffs of Kilnsey Crag, Knipe Scar and the scars of Grass Wood. Above this thick layer of pure limestone come a series of limestones with thin shales between them. These are the Yoredales,

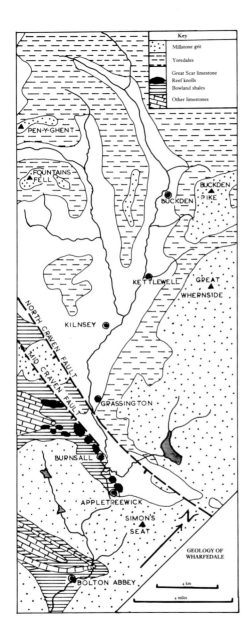

Key

	Millstone grit
	Yoredales
	Great Scar limestone
	Reef knolls
	Bowland shales
	Other limestones

GEOLOGY OF
WHARFEDALE

4 km

4 miles

after the old name for Wensleydale and the River Ure. There are four or five bands of limestone, each up to thirty feet (10m) thick, separated by thin shales and an occasional sandstone. These alternating limestones and shales exert a big influence on the scenery as they outcrop in dramatic fashion for miles along each side of Littondale, Wharfedale above Kettlewell, and along Langstrothdale like giant steps up to the moors above. The soft shales are easily weathered and form the flatter tread of the 'staircase'. The characteristic stepped scenery of Littondale did not escape the notice of the Rev Charles Kingsley when he wrote *The Water Babies* – little Tom had to jump down each great 'step' of limestone, one after the other, in order to reach the river below:

'Then he went down three hundred feet of limestone terraces, one below the other, as straight as if a carpenter had ruled them . . .

First, a little grass slope, covered with the prettiest flowers, rockrose and saxifrage, and thyme and basil . . .

Then bump down a two foot step of limestone.

Then another bit of grass and flowers.

Then bump down a one foot step.

Then another bit of grass and flowers for fifty yards, as steep as the house-roof . . .'

The Yoredale limestone is a little darker than the Great Scar and contains more fossils. Most of the fossil shells you are likely to see will be lampshells known as brachiopods, some of which are very large, like those at Mossdale Scar. Crinoid fragments are very common, and often thick slabs of limestone are made up entirely of their debris. A crinoid was an animal that grew on a stem attached to the seabed with long feathery arms that rose above it – hence its common name of sea-lily. You will see coral colonies too, looking

Terraces of the Yoredale series of rocks, outcropping above Dib Scar near Conistone.

rather like tubes of macaroni running through the rock.

Limestone Scenery The limestone has its own attractive scenery. Impressive white limestone scars and cliffs line the dale, the most outstanding of which are Kilnsey Crag with its distinctive shape and dramatic overhang, and Blue Scar in Littondale. The present dry valleys and ravines, like that at Conistone Dib (*walk 11*), were carved at the end of the Ice Age when torrents of meltwater swept down the valley sides and the ground below was still frozen hard.

When today's streams cross the limestone they disappear into sinks and reappear lower down as springs. Hell Hole near Trollers Gill (*walk 4*) swallows a small stream, and a large and impressive one disappears at Mossdale Scar (*walk 10*). Of the resurgent streams, the crystal-clear springs at the foot of Trollers Gill are remarkable, and further copious springs splash out in three or four places from below Kilnsey Crag (*walk 12*).

As you climb up out of the dale you will see some very fine sections of limestone pavements, such as those above Conistone (*walk 11*) where well-developed fissures or grikes shelter an interesting woodland vegetation. The grikes have dissolved along the natural joints in the rock which break it up into large cubes. The blocks of limestone are fretted and grooved by rainwater into wonderful pieces of natural sculpture. Such pavements occur where the limestone is bare and horizontal, having

3

been stripped of soil during the last advance of the ice. The purity of the limestone ensures that there is little mineral matter to form new soils. Where soils have become established, a short springy green turf full of wild flowers clothes the fells.

Underground Scenery The unique feature of limestone is that it is shaped and sculptured below ground as well as above. There are hundreds of depressions and round hollows on the surface. There are shakeholes – which are dry – and swallow holes or sinks, where water disappears beneath the surface, the 'pot holes' of the Dales.

It is perhaps surprising that such a seemingly hard rock like limestone can easily be dissolved by running water. Rainwater gathers a little carbon dioxide from the air and becomes slightly acidic. More acids are added from rotting plant remains in the soil, and water that has run off peaty soils is particularly active when it reaches the limestone, eating at it and carrying it away in solution. After heavy rain, water runs into joints and cracks, slowly dissolving and opening them up until eventually a new underground landscape of passages and caves is developed. Because caves open up along joints and horizontal bedding planes, they tend to have level passages linked to vertical clefts. They may contain rushing streams and waterfalls, or still pools and lakes with banks of sand and mud. The percolating water may then redeposit its rich solution of lime to form, in the total darkness, a wonderland of stalactites and stalagmites, of flowstone and rimstone pools, of pillars and straws.

Wharfedale has some of the most outstanding and beautiful caves in the country. On the eastern edge of the dale there is the fine show cave of Stump Cross Caverns which has four miles (6km) of passages, some of which are rich in beautiful stalagmite and pillar formations. Dow Cave near Kettlewell also provides magnificent cave scenery and is well-known and popular among cavers. Higher up the valley above Hubberholme is Strans Gill Pot, with its spectacularly decorated Passage of Time. In Littondale there is the almost inaccessible but decorated Boreham Cave and the nearby Scoska Cave, which has a wide entrance and can be visited by the adventurous walker. There are also dozens of others.

The Shales and Reef Knolls South of the Craven Fault The rocks south of the Craven Fault are quite different from those to the north, in that they are mainly mudstones and shales with only thin impure limestones. Also they have been strongly folded and fractured by earth movements. These are part of the unstable Craven Basin. The strata are four or five times as thick as the limestones to the north of the fault, and started being deposited earlier.

The Bowland shales can be seen by the river at Bolton Abbey and near Bolton Bridge (*walk 1*). Coiled goniatites, straight cones of a type of fossil nautilus, bivalves and fossil fish remains are preserved crushed in the shale, with occasional hard rounded lumps of limestone known as bullions embedded in the shales, which sometimes contain well-preserved fossils.

Along the line of the Craven Fault there is a fascinating line of knolls, beautiful green dome-shaped hills such as the two Kails, Elbolton, Stebden and Butter Haw which can be seen from several of the walks (*eg 4, 6, 7 and 8*). They are made of very pure limestone, rich in well-preserved fossils including even trilobites and goniatites, but mainly brachiopods (lampshells), gastropods (snails), bivalves (like clams and oysters), corals, bryozoans (these

4

Limestone reef knolls, and Thorpe Fell.

look like a piece of lace curtain) and crinoids (sea-lilies). All the debris from these animals built up into large mounds (or reefs) on the seabed of 330 million years ago and were eventually buried in mud. The mud became shale which has now largely weathered away, leaving the original

mounds exposed to view once again after 330 million years of burial. These hills could be the most ancient scenery that anyone has ever set eyes on! The rounded bright green knolls contrast beautifully with the dark sombre colours of Thorpe Fell behind them.

5

Some limestone fossils (left to right): crinoid stems, gigantoproductus, lithostrotion and small brachiopods.

The Skipton and Skyreholme Folds

Huge upfolds in the strata – known as anticlines – also add their influence to the scenery. The Skipton Anticline brought limestone up to the surface which otherwise would have been hidden deep below ground. This dark grey limestone is quarried at Haw Park in the core of the fold and there is a classic view of this anticline from Storiths Crag (*walk 1*). The limestones above and below the Cavendish Pavilion near Bolton Priory (*walk 2*) also belong to the centre of the same upfold. Higher up the dale, the limestone of Loup Scar on the Wharfe and that of Trollers Gill owes its presence to a parallel fold, the Skyreholme Anticline. This fold actually affects the strata on the north side of the Craven Fault

too, at Greenhow. These folds give an idea of the great forces generated in the crust during the earth movements which occurred at the end of the Carboniferous Period.

Millstone Grit Country The Grassington Grit is the lowest part of the larger Millstone Grit series. It is made up of thick sandstones and shales. The rough, coarse sandstone is known as gritstone or millstone grit. It occurs on both sides of the Craven Fault, on top of the Yoredale limestones to the north and on the Bowland Shales to the south.

The Grassington Grit caps the high fells between Littondale and Wharfedale, the higher peaks of Pen-y-ghent and Fountains Fell, as well as Buckden Pike and Great Whernside on the east side of the dale. Further south it is clearly seen on Barden Fell and Barden Moor. Stacks of rock such as Simon's Seat are a feature of these gritstone moors. The rock is a coarse, yellow-brown sandstone which contains large white or yellow quartz pebbles embedded in the rock, which weathers almost black. There are also layers of shale within it and, surprisingly, a coal seam, which has been mined on Threshfield and Grimwith Moors.

The darker grit moors contrast with the brighter green, short turf of limestone areas. Soils which develop on millstone grit are peaty and acid, lacking in calcium and not very fertile. They attract only a few species of plants so that one species may often dominate acres of moorland, such as the broad stretches of heather on the flat-topped moors, cotton grass on the higher fells, bilberry and crowberry round the rocky outcrops, or bracken on the steeper lower slopes.

Mineral Veins Soon after the rocks of Wharfedale were laid down, hot mineral fluids emanating from a granite mass, now centred 1,640 feet (500m) below Wensleydale and stretching as far south as Kettlewell, were injected into the surrounding strata. The fluids reacted with the limestone and crystallised as veins of calcite, barite or fluorite, with smaller amounts of galena, the ore of lead. The main orefields are on Grassington Moor (*walk 7*), Greenhow Hill, Appletreewick, Trollers Gill (*walk 4*), and the fells above Conistone (*walk 11*) and Buckden.

Glaciers and Rivers Ice covered much of Britain many times during the last two million years, and the last of these Ice Ages was at its peak 20,000 years ago. The Dales were then completely submerged under the ice, which was not only grinding down each dale but also riding over the tops of the fells, smoothing the landscape and carrying soil and debris with it to lower ground. By the action of the ice, Wharfedale gained its characteristic shape – a broad, straight, steep-sided, flat-floored, U-shaped valley, the textbook glacial trough.

About 15,000 years ago, when Wharfedale still had its own glacier, the climate became warmer and much of the ice melted in the summers, sending torrents of water along the edge of the valley glacier to form lakes in the side valleys. These lakes overflowed and the raging floodwaters cut channels which are now high on the valley sides. Five or six of these overflow channels today provide a strange landscape at Storiths opposite Bolton Priory (*walk 1*).

The material deposited at the snout of the glacier includes the mounds of stones and clay known as terminal moraines. The three in upper Wharfedale are at Skirfare Bridge, Chapel House and Drebley (*walk 4*), each of which may have formed a temporary dam holding back its own lake for a time after the ice had melted. Many side streams built up gravel fans where they entered the main valley, now the sites of villages at Buckden, Starbotton, Arncliffe, Kettlewell and Conistone.

On its journey through the Dales the ice carried a great many boulders, leaving them strewn about the hillsides, some perched high up like those above Trollers Gill. Others were carried into places where the rocks are of a different type, and these are known as erratics. Perhaps the most interesting of these are the slabs of ancient Silurian slate which can be found near Kilnsey. The ice gouged so deeply into the floor of the valley here that it took out a few blocks of the older rock, and then the site was covered up again by later debris. Pieces of the greenish-grey slate turn up in dry-stone walls below Kilnsey, where they make useful 'throughs' – these being the large stones that go through the wall from one side to the other and knit it together.

Perhaps the most important thing the ice did was to remove all the soil, so that modern soils have had only a short time to develop in what was once bare rock, and present soils are therefore thin and closely reflect the underlying geology. They are known as immature soils.

During the last 12,000 years the waters of the River Wharfe and its tributaries contributed further to our scenery by creating waterfalls, cutting deep gorges and forming river cliffs like Loup Scar (*walk 6*). In other places the river deposited sandy beaches and gravel patches like those at Bolton Abbey. And while this was going on the climate changed to a warmer one, and woodlands grew and clothed the landscape.

MAN AND THE LANDSCAPE

Before the arrival of man, Wharfedale was thickly wooded. It had swamps along the valley bottom, dense forests of oak, elm and alder, ash woods on the limestone, and a thinner woodland of hazel and birch on the higher ground. It was this primeval wooded landscape which man entered and settled. The high ridges became not only the easiest routeways but also the obvious places to live. The early settlers changed it only gradually to suit their needs, until over the last 1,000 years when the process was quickened.

Prehistoric man has left only a clue here and there of his existence, clues of a religious significance in the only henge, the remains of a chambered cairn and three small stone circles. A henge is an earthen circle and there is a fine example near Yarnbury (*walk 7*). The burial cairn is the Giant's Grave on Pen-y-ghent Gill (*walk 19*) and both of these are thought to be of late Neolithic age. The best stone circle is near Yockenthwaite and of the Bronze Age. Built of some twenty stones it measures twenty-five feet (7m) across (*walk 20*). Early man worked flakes of flint for use as scrapers, axes, arrow-heads and cutting implements, and bits of waste flint often turn up in molehills near some of these prehistoric sites. You can be sure that any piece of flint you may find has been brought into the dale and shaped or used by man. It is a type of rock alien to Wharfedale, and Neolithic tradesmen heaved it all the way from East Yorkshire where it occurs in the chalk. It was the raw material for making tools for thousands of years and was still in use throughout the Bronze Age (2,000-600 BC).

By about 600 BC the Bronze Age merged into the Iron Age with the arrival of groups of Celts from the Continent. Among them, some time in the third century BC, came the Brigantes from the Lake Constance area to occupy a large part of the North of England. These people bred horses and cattle, and were highly skilled and artistic in the working of metal. They had iron ploughs and axes which were more efficient than flint. Larger clearings could be made for their circular, stone-based wooden huts with skins and thatch for the roof, and for the small rectangular fields they ploughed for crops of primitive wheat. There are many Iron Age fields and hut circles on the higher ground, with a fine example at Dew Bottoms on the Monk's Road (*walk 18*). Some of the finest 'Celtic fields' in Britain are near Grassington (*walk 10*). You can see them best in the light of the evening sun or after a dusting of snow.

The Romans arrived in Britain in AD 43, and by AD 71, as they forced their way north with the help of the first-ever network of good roads, they had conquered the Vale of York. They forged a route through Wharfedale over Stake Moss to Bainbridge in Wensleydale. A small part of the Roman road can be seen today north of Buckden (*walk 17*). In AD 74 the Romans subdued the Brigantes of the area, who had resisted by building the massive wall of Tor Dike above Kettlewell (*walk 13*), as well as the stone fort at Fort Gregory in Grass Wood. These fortifications defended Brigantian strongholds to the north and west. We know that the Romans mined lead at Greenhow and probably used Brigantes as slaves in the mines. Eventually the local people lived at peace with their invaders, traded with them in meat and wool, and intermarriages took place.

The Romans had left by AD 410, and some of the Romano-Britons continued on their hill farms while others cleared new land on the valley floor. The Celtic 'kingdom' of Craven was established, which included upper Wharfedale. Craven is one of the very few Celtic names that remain – meaning 'the land of wild garlic'. The fair-haired Angles came to the Dales about the year 620. (They came from an area which is now northern Germany.) These immigrants were lowland farmers who led a communal way of life, clearing more of the woodland, tilling the common ground on the valley slopes and ploughing strips of land.

The modern pattern of compact villages in upper Wharfedale is a direct reflection of Anglian settlement in the seventh century. Attractive village greens are a reminder of how the Anglian community kept livestock in safety at the centre of the village, surrounded by their homesteads. Over the years, village greens have been the hub of community life, where water was carried from the village pump, where farm animals and foodstuffs were bought and sold, and where travelling shows were held. There are large attractive greens in Arncliffe and Linton, and smaller ones in Conistone and Thorpe.

The Danes came mainly to the lower dales. In the late ninth century, after destroying many early villages and churches, some reached upper Wharfedale and settled at Thorpe and Burnsall (*walk 6*). They were lowland farmers like the Angles and merged in with them. A century later the Norse Vikings landed on the western shores of Cumbria and Lancashire, and established individual farmsteads in the unoccupied land at the head of the dale. They were independent sheep farmers and, being used to life in the mountains of Norway, they preferred the higher fell country where there was grazing land. They did not live in villages but on unsettled land at the upper part of

Wharfedale at Cray (*walk 17*), Kirk Gill, Raisgill, Yockenthwaite and Beckermonds (*walk 20*). It was these Norsemen who brought a great influence on the language of the Dales. Along with some Anglian words, the basis of the Yorkshire dialect had been laid down by the time of the Norman conquest.

Place names are a good clue as to the origin of early settlements. Early Anglian (English) names often contain *ing*, meaning the 'place of so-and-so', as in Grassington and Hartlington. The villages in clearings are those ending in *ley*, such as Drebley. The suffix *ton* refers to a farmstead, for example Starbotton, Litton and Linton. Danish names included *thorp*, as in Thorpe near Burnsall, meaning an outlying hamlet. *Thwaite* – a clearing – is of Norse origin, and many of the names for the physical landscape come from the Norse, such as dale, beck, crag, fell, gill, moss and scar, which are reminiscent of Lakeland names and the Norse settlement there.

From 1066 troubled times ensued in the north of England. The Normans were not immigrants like the Angles and the Danes, but came as fighters and conquerers. The local people rebelled. There was a great deal of destruction in the 'Harrying of the North' and large numbers of the population were slaughtered. In Wharfedale, hunting forests were reserved for the new Norman lords such as the Romilles and the Percys.

Perhaps the biggest influence on the landscape of Wharfedale came with the growth and power of the monasteries. In 1155, Alice de Romille gave land for the founding of Bolton Priory (*walk 1*). She also donated land at Kilnsey to Fountains Abbey, twenty-five miles (40km) away to the west, so Wharfedale became part monastic and part hunting estate. Fountains Fell still carries the name of the abbey. Bolton Priory came to own a great deal of land, with property far beyond Wharfedale.

The ancient medieval field system: lynchets, below reef knolls and Thorpe Fell.

The monasteries developed vast sheep ranches, with drove roads and a chain of farms and granges. The production of wool was the wealth of the land, but the rearing of sheep came to have a devastating effect on the landscape. Young seedling trees could not survive the grazing sheep, and in time, older trees died off so that big areas of upland became treeless grasslands. The scenery was changing dramatically.

In the late medieval period, there developed the terraces or lynchets which can be seen as you go up the dale. It was easier to plough in one direction so that soil was turned down the slope. Generations of ploughing in this way, and the placing of stones on the edge of the strip, produced the terraces. They form large 'steps' in the fields, especially near Burnsall (*walk 6*) and Threshfield (*walk 8*).

The monasteries created a market for grain, meat, linen, and boots and shoes. Local people prospered and villages began to grow, Grassington and Kettlewell becoming early trading centres. Many new roads and trackways were established across the dale as monastic trade grew between Ribblesdale and Wensleydale. Mastiles Lane, which passed the grange at Kilnsey (*walk 12*), and the Monk's Road through Arncliffe (*walk 18*) are both part of this network. In the villages the presence of a church reflected the growing population, and the earliest stone churches are those of Linton, Burnsall and Conistone, which date from the twelfth century.

The Scots raids continued throughout the monastic age, penetrating deep into Craven. Crops were set on fire, animals stolen, and on more than one occasion the canons of the priory had to find shelter further south. In 1513, under Henry Clifford, the Dalesmen fought back at Flodden Field. Weapons used at the battle were brought back to show children, and one of the pikes hangs on the wall in Arncliffe Church.

The dissolution of Bolton Priory came in 1539 along with other monasteries, and wealth and power went to new landowners, with the establishment of big private estates, like the one which has passed down to the present Duke of Devonshire. The building of stone farmhouses began about 1600, replacing wattle and daub and thatch, so most early domestic buildings in

A typical Dales barn with accommodation for a farm hand.

12

upper Wharfedale are seventeenth century – a period the historian W G Hoskins called 'the Great Rebuild' – and include schools, manor houses, halls, inns, farmhouses and bridges.

Burnsall Grammar School was built in 1602 and that at Threshfield in 1675 (*walk 8*), and both are still in use today as schools. Many fine halls and manor houses date from this period. Low Hall at Appletreewick was built in 1658 and the New Hall in 1667 (*walk 4*). Kilnsey Old Hall (*walk 12*) is inscribed 'CW 1648' and was once a fine house visited by Lady Anne Clifford in 1663 (it now serves as a barn). Many smaller houses and cottages throughout the dale are of the same period and, as you walk past, notice the dates over the doors.

The typical Dales farmhouse is long and narrow in plan, with living accommodation and animals all under one low flagstone roof. The farmhouses have vertical stone divisions, or mullions, between the window panes and often a dated lintel above the door, usually with the initials of the original farmer and his wife carved on it. Good examples can be seen especially in the upper parts of Wharfedale and Littondale (*walks 17 and 20*). The farmhouse was divided into kitchen and parlour, with a connecting door through to the animals. Later a porch was added to the front door, and an offshut or lean-to along the length of the building at the back for a kitchen and a dairy.

Scattered field barns are as much a part of the scenery of the dale as the villages, and many of them were built in the seventeenth and eighteenth centuries. Most housed four or five cows in the winter, which were fed on the hay stored in the loft. The barns – or laithes as they are known – were of a standard plan; the roofs are of flagstone, but some old ones with steeply pitched roofs were originally thatched with ling gathered from the moor. Bridges in the dale are fine monuments to the people who built them, and it is a wonder how they take the heavy modern traffic. A sixteenth century packhorse bridge can be seen in Linton village. The ancient bridge at Grassington was built in 1603 and has withstood the worst of the floods (*walk 9*); it was widened in the eighteenth century when the road became a turnpike from Skipton to Pateley Bridge. Bolton Bridge was rebuilt after flood damage in 1673 (*walk 1*), along with the magnificent bridge at Barden (*walk 2*) which was used by Lady Anne Clifford on her journeys north. The graceful bridge at Burnsall was rebuilt in 1884 (*walk 6*), replacing Sir William Craven's bridge of 1602.

The stone walls which cover the valleys in an intricate network are an outstanding and characteristic feature of the Yorkshire Dales. They occasionally run up the slopes and over the tops in a seemingly endless maze. In the sunshine they stand out as a pattern of strong lines and shadows in the landscape. There are gritstone walls and limestone walls, and a sudden change from one to the other reflects a change in the underlying geology. They were built without mortar and are known as drystone walls.

Some walls, near to villages, where they surround small, irregularly-shaped fields, are of the sixteenth and early seventeenth century, built by the more wealthy farmers as they took in some of the common land. The main wall-building period, known as 'the Enclosures', was between 1780 and 1820, when it became law to enclose all private land. The straight geometrical shapes of fields of this period are well seen near Conistone (*walk 11*). Drove roads and packhorse tracks were preserved and became the walled green roads of today (*walks 10 and 12*). Arthur Raistrick records that a good wall-builder could put up seven yards of wall a day - which works out as

Barden Bridge.

lifting twelve tons of stone! The wallers were skilled workmen and the craft is carried on today with the encouragement of walling competitions such as that at the Kilnsey Show.

Many old limekilns are also part of the dales scenery, with over 700 in the National Park (*walks 10 and 12*). They were in use in the eighteenth and nineteenth centuries to convert limestone into lime. The main use of the lime was to improve the fertility of the land by sweetening acid soils, but it was also needed to make mortar for building. The basic structure of the field kiln is a squarish tower set into the hillside, which contained a sandstone-lined bowl, tapering at the base, where the burnt lime and ashes were raked out through an archway. A lot of farmland in the valley bottom was improved by draining and liming.

The beauty of Wharfedale was little affected by the important leadmining industry, which flourished from the seventeenth century until about 1880, since it was carried out high up on the moors. Scores of mines and spoil heaps remain at Yarnbury (*walk 7*), Greenhow, Appletreewick (*walk 4*), Capplestone Gate (*walk 11*) and Buckden (*walk 16*). Smelt mills were in use on Grassington Moor, at Conistone, Linton and Hebden, and traces may also be found of the sites of water wheels, chimneys and flues.

Of no recent invention are the miles of enticing footpaths, of which the walker is making ever-increasing use. They reflect centuries of movement of people on foot from one place to another. On foot along the parishioners' ways to church; on foot along the ancient monks' trails from one dale to the next; on foot along drove roads across the country; on foot on packhorse tracks to and from old mines; or just simply on foot by villagers' ways over stiles and through fields to the next village. The whole network of footpaths is a most

A disused limekiln at Cote Gill, Littondale.

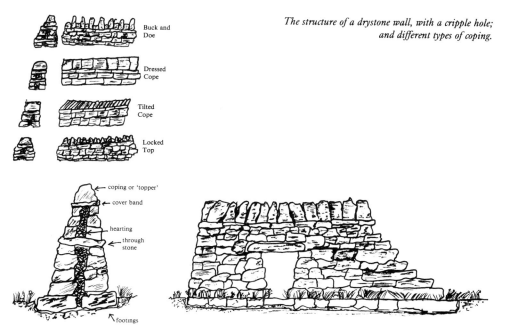

*The structure of a drystone wall, with a cripple hole;
and different types of coping.*

Buck and
Doe

Dressed
Cope

Tilted
Cope

Locked
Top

coping or 'topper'

cover band

hearting

through
stone

footings

valuable legacy to be used and preserved for present and future generations of walkers in the Dales.

The duty of the National Park authority, with help from other groups, is to protect the natural beauty of the dales and its cultural heritage. But there are many pressures which threaten the landscape.

Quarrying is a major concern, and there are three commercial limestone quarries in upper Wharfedale. The one at Swinden is the biggest and makes use of the railway line which between 1902 and 1930 carried passengers to Grassington. The quarry is gradually removing the pure limestone of a large reef knoll, forming a huge scar on the landscape and creating problems of noisy machinery and of dust covering the surrounding countryside. The quarries at Skirethorns and Kilnsey are more hidden from view, but the steady removal of entire hillsides still continues within the National Park, and much of this chemically pure limestone is only used for roadstone.

Changes in farming methods are also having an effect on the landscape. Intensive farming entails the use of fertilisers, draining wet land and reseeding fields, which result in loss of the wild flowers, insect and birdlife. Making silage in May instead of haymaking in June or July does not give time for flowers to set seed before being cut, and again results in loss of wild flowers. Field barns and walls have fallen out of use and are crumbling through neglect. However, steps have been taken to reverse these trends. By voluntary agreement with farmers, a large part of upper Wharfedale has been made an ESA – environmentally sensitive area – which involves following guidelines designed to protect the countryside. This, together with a scheme for the conservation of barns and walls, is proving very successful.

One other pressure which won't go away is people! Nearly 10,000,000 people visit the National Park every year, with the accompanying problems of too much traffic along the narrow roads and of erosion on popular footpaths. Both are being tackled through the National Park Committee.

What will the landscape look like in the twenty-first century? A joint study by the National Park and the University of East Anglia culminated in the exhibition *Landscapes for Tomorrow* which toured the villages in 1990. Will it be a wilderness landscape, an intensively farmed landscape or a specially-cared-for conservation landscape? The future of the landscape is the concern and responsibility not only of the administrators but also of the visitors, and the people who live and work there too.

WILDLIFE

In the days of the old hunting forests, eagles, merlins, and buzzards were common in upper Wharfedale – and in fact the name Arncliffe means 'eagle's cliff'. In the fifteenth century, abbey servants were paid three shillings a week to keep watch over the sheep on Fountains Fell and guard against wolves. In the seventeenth century there were still herds of red deer on the fells, otters swam in the Wharfe and pine martens lived in the woodland.

Time has produced new residents. At the turn of the century the oystercatcher was a rare visitor, but is now a common breeding bird. Even more recently, the goosander was a rare winter visitor but now breeds regularly along the Wharfe. Wild mink, descendants of escapees from fur farms, have found a habitat to their liking along the river.

Upper Wharfedale is exceptional in possessing a wide variety of habitats for birds. Well-known is the stretch of broadleaved woodland along the river above Bolton Abbey. This provides nest-sites for many species. High above are some of the best grouse moors in the country. The river itself and tributary streams support a rich birdlife. There are in addition many other habitats in the farmland, ash woods, limestone pastures and scars, young forest plantations, high peaks and bogs and the freshwater reservoirs of Grimwith and Barden. Here are some favourite bird-watching localities:

The River Wharfe From Barden to Grassington (walks 2, 4 and 6) The river is still youthful and vigorous along this stretch, and varies considerably in its mood.

There are falls and rapids, shallows and pools, water rushing over stones and boulders, and quiet stretches where the river runs deep. This is all attractive habitat for many riverside birds. The mallard is everywhere and also, in smaller numbers, is the more secretive moorhen. The goosander has bred here for only the last twenty years as its breeding range edges southwards, but is a bird you are very likely to see.

You are also likely to see the dipper, a small sturdily-built bird with a white front, bobbing and dipping as it stands on a stone in the river, or as it flies straight and low over the water with whirring wings. So too the pied wagtail, which can be seen in a wide variety of habitats and – like its cousin the grey wagtail – prefers good open space around it so that it can keep an eye open for predators. The colourful grey wagtail has striking yellow underparts and seeks its prey near rushing water, often in the company of the dipper. The most handsome of all is the kingfisher, also a resident, which nests in a hole in the bank. You may see it first as a flash of blue as it flies from one perch to another, watching for small fish through the moving surface of the water.

Among the summer visitors, another hole-dweller is the sand martin which arrives by the end of March. It uses nesting sites of the previous year in the sandy parts of the riverbank. Two weeks later the martins are joined by the common sandpiper, heralding its arrival with a shrill piping call. A favourite place for these two is just above Barden Bridge.

The woods at Bolton Abbey (walks 1 and 2) The extensive woodland of Bolton Woods and Strid Wood clothes the banks of the Wharfe for some two and a half miles (4½ km) upstream from Bolton Abbey. There is a mixture of mainly oak, beech and

sycamore with some birch and conifers, including mature and young trees. Wildlife conservation is actively promoted throughout the Bolton Abbey estate. Rotting branches are left to provide habitats for insects – and thereby food for birds – and new plantings are planned to balance the attraction of wildlife with timber production.

It is worth a visit to Bolton Woods at any time of year, but the end of April and the beginning of May is the best time, before the leaves are fully out on the trees and after the arrival of most of the summer species. At this time the birds are paired in their own territories, and you can hear them call and see them displaying, preparing their nests and feeding their young. About fifty different species breed here annually, and with patience it should be possible to see a good proportion of these. One of the most popular is the pied fly-catcher, which nests in a hole in a tree usually near the river. Something like twenty pairs breed annually. Its cousin the spotted flycatcher may be seen as it dashes out to catch a favourite fly, then returns to its perch again.

Of the warblers, the willow warbler is the most common and is identified by its melodious descending notes. The wood warbler's song contains rapid trills and the blackcap pours out a beautiful warbling song, usually from dense cover near the nest. The secretive garden warbler requires plenty of undergrowth for a nest site near the ground. Its song is an endless, sweeter, lower-pitched warble than the blackcap, whereas the chiffchaff likes a high perch to deliver its monotonous 'chiff-chaff'. Stand quietly and listen. Some of them will be around. You might see a redstart flashing its red tail, or a tree pipit parachuting down to a solitary tree in a clearing.

Resident birds include the woodcock, which in spring can be seen at dusk from the Cavendish Pavilion on its 'roding' flight. This is the name given to the bird's backward and forward flight in the darkening sky above the tree tops. The great spotted woodpecker is attracted to dead boughs, and green woodpeckers give themselves away by their laughing call. Nuthatches and tree creepers are present throughout the year. In winter, parties of

Treecreeper.

long-tailed tits move through the trees, as well as groups of blue, great and coal tits, often accompanied by a marsh tit or one or two goldcrests. The day-flying little owl and the nocturnal tawny owl both breed in the woods. On the fringes of the woodland keep your eyes open for the sparrowhawk, for this is where it likes to hunt, swooping through the trees hoping to grasp some unwary bird.

18

Grimwith Reservoir (walk 5) Man-made reservoirs continue to provide essential habitats for waterfowl and waders, which otherwise face a steady decline in their natural wetland environment. The recently expanded 370 acre (150ha) reservoir at Grimwith is no exception. It is now the biggest inland water in Yorkshire and was officially opened in 1985. It replaced the former reservoir, built in Victorian times, which was also of some importance for water birds. At the northern end there are some mudflats on the shores which become more extensive at low water in the summer. It is here that the two streams, Blae Beck and Gate Up Beck, enter the lake. The new reservoir – like the old – is attracting numbers of interesting waterbirds, and many of them have found breeding and feeding grounds at this northern section, which is where they tend to congregate.

The large and striking Canada geese are sociable birds, and a flock of over a hundred with their young gathers in the summer months to graze on the banks. In the breeding season they become particularly noisy, with a trumpeting 'ka-honk' flight call. For the ringed plover this is the only breeding place in Wharfedale. It may be distinguished from the little ringed plover by the larger size, deeper orange legs and bill, and the white wing bar when seen in flight. Herons and redshank both frequent the shore. The heron likes any watery habitat where the fishing is good, and is most active at dawn and dusk. The redshank is also at home on open pastures. Teal is our smallest species of duck and from a distance the male appears to have a

Ringed plover.

Pied flycatcher.

dark head and pale body. They nest in boggy parts of the moor away from the water. Wigeon have bred at Grimwith for many years and are re-establishing themselves on the new reservoir, which is one of their few breeding places outside Scotland. You can distinguish them by the chestnut and cream head of the male. In winter you are likely to see another handsome duck, the goldeneye, which looks black above and white below. They are tireless divers and are most at home in the water.

The rough grassland round Grimwith (walk 5) Birds typical of rough grassland are found around the shores of Grimwith. This area is 1,000 feet (300m) high up on the Pennines on millstone grit terrain, which here rises to heather moors to the north and west. The most common bird is the meadow pipit. In summer they display by rising from the ground in a song flight, climbing into the air and gliding down again with wings down and tail up. Over the drier pastures, skylarks hover in continuous song. Parties of twite, with prominent white flashes in wings and tail, especially noticeable in flight, can be seen feeding on the many thistle heads in the summer. The snipe likes very wet land and, when flushed, dashes up with a screech and a zigzagging flight. The kestrel may be seen hovering above its hunting ground at any time of year. The curlew, which likes the damper areas, gives its wild haunting call from February onwards, adding a bubbling version as the breeding season begins. Lapwings also arrive by the end of February to find suitable habitat for nesting. Reed buntings, too, are resident at Grimwith. The small whinchat takes up its territory in the summer after its long flight from south of the Sahara. Look out, too, for the blue-grey stockdove which also inhabits this area, and in the rocky places the shy ring ouzel. Starlings and pied wagtails nest among rocks, in walls or around old buildings, and the migrant wheatear finds a rocky hole or makes use of an old rabbit burrow.

Pen-y-ghent and Fountains Fell (walk 19) To survive on the high tops, birds need to be particularly hardy. Both the dunlin and the golden plover occur here. The dunlin is the smallest of our breeding waders and is a common shore bird. The golden plover is a favourite of the upland parts of the Dales with its distinguished black and gold back, and in summer its black underparts. The song is a liquid whistle and a mournful call note, and this bird is likely to be heard before being seen. The peregrine hunts over the fells and it is worth looking skywards for a sign of it. On the sides of Pen-y-ghent you may get a visit from the raven as it glides past with a deep grunting croak and long, finger-like primary feathers at its wing tips. The snow bunting may be seen in summer – the lucky few may spot a party of snow buntings in the winter with their characteristic flash of white wings.

Valley farmland between Barden and Burnsall (walks 2 and 4) Pheasants are very common near Barden – particularly before the shooting season begins in October – and many get killed by traffic on the road. It is the handsome male which delivers the raucous crow. As well as on higher pastures, the lapwing also nests on rough farmland. It looks black and white from a distance, but its distinctive greenish back and long whispy crest makes it an attractive bird. Glossy-black, palefaced rooks nest in colonies in the tops of tall trees, while the smaller, grey-headed jackdaw likes old farm buildings, ruins and cliffs.

Swallows nest in farm buildings and often return year after year to the same site. The less common seed-eating yellowhammer is another inhabitant of farmland. It takes up a territory along the hedgerows, from which it delivers its 'little-bit-of-bread-and-no-cheese' song. The bright yellow wing-flashes and white rump of the goldfinch distinguish this bird in flight, but it is a delight to see parties of them feeding on thistle seeds in the late summer. Pied wagtails hunt for flies not only along the river but also in farmyards, and they will also follow grazing sheep for the insects which they disturb. In the autumn, migrant redwings and fieldfares occur in flocks, feeding on berry-bearing bushes or probing for worms in the grass.

The heather moors of Barden Fell and Barden Moor (walks 2 and 3) Heather is both home and food for the red grouse – without it the bird cannot exist. To ensure a good grouse population the heather has to be properly managed by burning selected areas. This produces young plants with nutritious green shoots adjacent to the mature heather needed for cover and nesting sites. On the heather moors, too, as well as on other rough pastures, are the meadow pipits. Preying on them are still a few merlins, but it will be a fortunate walker who sees one. Exploiting them in a different way in May and June is the cuckoo, as the meadow pipit is the most common species to be 'cuckolded'. On the bracken-clad slopes, the sprightly whinchat 'tacks' away at you for daring to go near.

Although the golden plover inhabits the high fells, where the vegetation is more sparse, it never seems to be far from heather and it will often remain within view, its golden plumage shining in the summer sun. One of the greatest delights of a moorland walk is to see the short-eared owl slowly flapping over its territory, keeping low over the heather as it hunts for voles. Another bird of the moors is the black-headed gull. A huge nesting colony is to be found by the upper reservoir on Barden Moor. The lesser black-backed gull and a few Canada geese also breed here.

Limestone pastures and scars round Trollers Gill (walk 4) The lapwing, peewit or green plover (the three names taken together define the bird without possibility of error) can be seen every-where. It might even come and attack if you get too near its nest. That wader with red legs and bill, the redshank, is also present. It is easily recognised by its mournful and distinctive 'tu-tu-tu' call. Around the rocks, both on limestone and gritstone, look out for the wheatear, a cocky little bird with a white rump which it displays as it flies away. In the gill itself and near Hell Hole is another habitat of the ring ouzel. Its monotonous call of 'tac-tac-tac-tac' may give it away. You may be fortunate to see the male snipe 'drumming', an astonishing diving display with tail outspread. The quivering outer tail feathers vibrate to produce a resonant beating sound as the bird sideslips through the air.

There are many other kinds of wildlife in the dale:

Mammals When walking in Wharfe-dale you will never be without wildlife for long, though some of the more secretive inhabitants may seldom allow themselves to be seen. In spite of its persecution by keepers, the handsome fox still manages to survive and is just as much at home on the mountain side as down in the valley or near human habitation. Its thick bushy tail, often white-tipped, is distinctive. They are wary animals and have an acute sense of hearing and smell. In rabbit country along the drystone walls lives the slim and active stoat. Light brown in colour, it is an in-quisitive animal and often sits up to look around, revealing its creamy white under-side. The head and body measure ten inches (25cm) long and the black-tipped tail an additional three (7½ cm). Another carnivore and cousin of the stoat is the mink, which likes to be near water. After being introduced into Britain from North America for its fur in the 1920s, it soon spread into the wild and is still extending its range. Mink are dark brown in colour, have a bushy tail and are half as big again as a stoat.

In the woods between Bolton Abbey and Barden lives the small roe deer. Two feet (60cm) high at the shoulder, the male has only short antlers, which are cast in November or December. The summer coat is a sleek, foxy red but by October turns to a thick, dark brown. The white rump is distinctive as it bounds away.

Reptiles Adders are very timid and rarely seen – Barden Moor is the only

easterly direction, and away to the left towards Ilkley and Otley. Straight ahead the twin gritstone edges of Skipton Moor and Thorpe Fell face each other on the skyline, and between them the limestone hump of Haw Park, its dark limestone rapidly being quarried away for roadstone. The view is of the Skipton Anticline – a textbook example of an upfold in the strata.

Nearby the low hillocks of Storiths can clearly be seen. The dips between them, now occupied by the farmhouses, are channels formed by glacial meltwater trapped between the Wharfedale glacier and the hillside. Towards the end of the Ice Age the rushing water spilled across this ridge of land, cutting successively lower channels. The ridge was carved into the present row of knolls, a feature that can be seen from miles around.

Dipper.

Bolton Priory

33

Passing Town End Farm, the path enters the access area of Barden Fell, part of the estate of the Duke of Devonshire and managed by the Chatsworth Trust. An information board has a map and gives the bylaws, one of which is 'no dogs'. The laws are designed to protect the grouse shooting —another forbids the flying of kites which grouse could mistake for a bird of prey and possibly panic unnecessarily.

From here the route is signposted and most of the way it is a double track. Three outlying farms of Storiths are passed lower down on the left, two of which were once lived in by Petty families. Ahead a completely new vista of moorland reveals itself, where kestrels hunt over the heather and red grouse warn you to 'go back'.

The soils are acid on the millstone grit moors and the vegetation is restricted in the number of species which grow, so large areas become dominated by one type. The broad stretches of purple heather are in flower in August and early September, transforming the colour of the moor top. Heather is encouraged by controlled burning, as the young shoots are the main food for the grouse. Bracken is found on the steeper slopes where gravity mixes the soils, making them richer and deeper: 'under bracken gold, under heather silver'. However, bracken is poisonous and is generally avoided by sheep, so it is not a favourite plant of either the farmer or the keeper. It does makes good cover for meadow pipits and in summer for whinchats and twite. Bracken is fast growing and can reach shoulder height by midsummer, its colour changing with the season from bright to dark green, then the coppery reds and golds of autumn.

After crossing Pickles Gill the path leads up through the bracken, with fine views across to Airedale and Pendle Hill. Branching left at the next junction of tracks continue to Hammerthorn Gate and climb

over the high stone stile, stepping on one of the old bench marks. The Ordnance Survey used the broad arrow and a brass pin to denote a certain height above sea level. Later bench marks are carved on a vertical surface with the government arrow and a horizontal line above it. Bench marks and their heights are printed on old 'six inch' maps. Walk down through the scattered oak trees of the former deer park to Bolton Park Farm and the wooden bridge over the river.

The Cavendish Pavilion is a good stopping point. There are always some mallard which congregate near the pavilion hoping for scraps of food. From the bridge you may catch sight of a dipper as it bobs and curtsies, along with the pied wagtails, on boulders in the river. A close view of the dipper may reveal a white blinking of its eyes. This bird is an ornithological curiosity in having a unique membrane over its eyes, which it opens and closes to clean them. From here to Bolton Bridge the route follows the Dales Way. Continue on the left bank to the end of the field. Join the road for a few yards and for the second time the route fords Pickles Gill. This beck is where the mink likes to make its home. They are normally dark brown, about 16 inches (40cm) long and are never far from water. They eat fish and waterfowl, and are regularly trapped on the Bolton Abbey estate as they pose a threat to other wildlife. All the wild mink are descended from animals that escaped from fur farms.

From here go up the road a few paces and follow the signpost through the woods to the right. This is a most beautiful woodland walk amidst mature beeches on a gallery footpath high above the river. In the spring there are masses of wood anemones and bluebells. On a summer evening the air is scented with the sweet smell of honeysuckle, and the foxglove is in flower. The path forks further on, but either way will bring you down to the river and to the footbridge opposite the priory. If the water is low you will be able to see the old stepping stones. Downstream is a view of the high shale cliffs, from the top of which there is a striking view of the priory, seen earlier in the walk. The Bolton Abbey Fault divides the Bowland shales on the left from the grits on the right.

Take time to wander through the lovely grounds of Bolton Priory. The priory was founded by Augustinian canons who moved here in 1155, but it was dissolved in 1539 with the tower still incomplete. The last prior was Richard Moone, and families with the name of Moon and Hey have lived in nearby Beamsley village for generations. Here originated the old nursery rhyme:

'HEY diddle, diddle, the cat and the fiddle,
The cow jumped over the MOON.'

The Heys were a family of wheelwrights, though never quite so well-to-do as the related Moons. The nave of the original church was fortunately saved, as it had to be used as the parish church. The picturesque ruins are of various periods, and the beauty of Bolton Priory has attracted many famous painters and poets. Ruskin introduced Turner, the great British painter, to this area and both Turner and Landseer made important paintings of the abbey, while Wordworth's poem the *White Doe of Rylstone* was inspired by his visit here.

Continue down the right bank of the river, to a point about halfway to Bolton Bridge where some shale outcrops in the river bed, a place where recently a Bradford schoolboy found a fossil fish. It turned out to be one of a group of small marine fish, a fast-moving predator with sharp teeth, which lived in shallow coastal seas some 330 million years ago. The fossil consisted only of the shiny black head-plates and jaws so small that the whole fish would have been only an inch or so (3 cm) long. The shales here also contain the shells of a mussel-like bivalve – seen as many whitish marks on the rock – as well as the spiral imprints of goniatites, which not only confirm the marine origin but date the rock as Upper Bowland shale. In amongst the shales are several large 'bullions', huge round symmetrical boulders two or three feet across. These concentrations of lime within the shales are very hard and brittle, and occasionally contain well-preserved fossils.

Traditionally, at the end of June 1644, Prince Rupert and his 18,000 royalist men camped in these fields, trampling a crop of corn that was shortly to be harvested. It was the Civil War and they were on their way to Marston Moor near York, where the battle took place on the 2nd July, leaving 3,000 of them dead. They were routed by Fairfax and his Yorkshire army with Cromwell and others in the great parliamentary victory. It is just a short stride from here to Bolton Bridge.

WALK 2: THE VALLEY OF DESOLATION AND SIMON'S SEAT

Start: Cavendish Pavilion, Bolton Abbey. Grid Ref: 077 553
Distance: 8½ miles (14km)
OS Maps: Outdoor Leisure 10 or Landranger 104
Walking Time: 4½ hours.

This is one of Wharfedale's classic walks and has been written about on many occasions. It is excellent for river and woodland birds and wild flowers. This makes a fine full day's excursion, but give yourself plenty of time to enjoy it. To arrive at the start of the walk, turn right off the B6160 near the Cavendish Memorial, Bolton Abbey. There is a charge for parking at the Cavendish Pavilion or by the river.

From the Cavendish Pavilion cross the wooden bridge and turn upstream through the stile. At the end of this field, note that the limestone in the riverbank here is almost vertical. It has been strongly folded and lies near the centre line of the Skipton Anticline.

Round the corner and facing upstream is a small cave worth exploring known as Dob Stream Cave. Make your way round the water's edge on the upturned edges of the limestone rocks to the hidden entrance. This was a trial adit – a horizontal tunnel – for lead and is perfectly safe to enter. The white mineral calcite outcrops at the mouth of the cave and shows why the miners tunnelled here in their search for galena, the

Simon's Seat, with Trollers Gill to its left, from Barden Moor.

valuable ore of lead, which they failed to find. In the early summer this is a good area to see the bright purplish flowers of wood cranesbill.

Go up the steps to the road, and a few paces higher up cross onto a small path parallel to the road. The wood here in spring is a mass of bluebells. At the brow of the hill, go through the gate which leads into the access area and a second gate. This is an old deer park with scattered ancient oaks, though no deer have been kept here since 1914. In 1980, members of the Ramblers Association planted 100 new young oak trees, many of which are growing well. Oak trees and oak woods tend to be very rich in wildlife and this has been born out by a study of the number of insects living on various woodland trees, the oak having nearly 300 species whereas the sycamore, for example, has only 15. Of course the high number of insects acts as a magnet for birds and mammals.

Keep to the left to enter the Valley of Desolation and to visit the waterfall in Posforth Gill. The route straight on up the hill passes by the landslip and descends to the stream above the falls. The landslip is in glacial debris, and occurred about fifteen years ago following heavy rain. Trees have been planted to prevent further erosion. In spite of this small scar, the Valley of Desolation is now a misnomer since it was

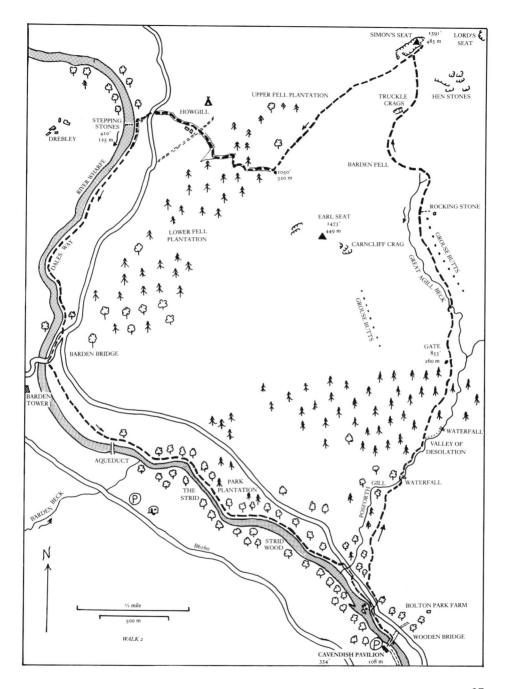

SIMON'S SEAT 1591' 485 m LORD'S SEAT

UPPER FELL PLANTATION

TRUCKLE CRAGS

HEN STONES

HOWGILL

STEPPING STONES 410' 125 m

DREBLEY

BARDEN FELL

1050' 320 m

ROCKING STONE

LOWER FELL PLANTATION

EARL SEAT 1473' 449 m

CARNCLIFF CRAG

GROUSE BUTTS

GREAT AGILL BECK

BARDEN BRIDGE

GROUSE BUTTS

GATE 853' 260 m

BARDEN TOWER

AQUEDUCT

WATERFALL

VALLEY OF DESOLATION

THE STRID

PARK PLANTATION

BARDEN BECK

GILL WATERFALL

P

B6160

STRID WOOD

POSFORTH

N

½ mile

500 m

WALK 2

BOLTON PARK FARM

WOODEN BRIDGE

P

CAVENDISH PAVILION 354' 108 m

as long ago as 1826 that a violent storm destroyed many of the trees here and the place became 'desolate'. You can still pick out one or two gnarled, ancient 'blasted oaks' and a few more recent dead elms, victims of Dutch Elm disease. But today, this hidden glen has regrown into one of the most attractive spots in Wharfedale.

Posforth Gill in winter.

Cross the stream below the falls and climb the shelf of gritstone which marks the fifty foot (15m) high waterfall. A variety of spring flowers grow here and in the summer there is a great display of foxgloves. Butterflies include the elusive green hairstreak which can be seen in May. It is a tiny butterfly that looks brown until it lands, when it shows the green underside of the wings. The brightly coloured small copper and green-veined white also frequent this area. Just over the wooden footbridge on the other side of the stream is a small spring with watercress and opposite-leaved golden saxifrage. The latter, although it forms greenish-yellow mats of colour, is a flower without petals. On the left of the path, two groups of giant horsetails are growing strongly. These plants often indicate a calcareous spring. They are very primitive and are related to the much bigger specimens of 300 million years ago in the Coal Measure forests. Those primeval specimens grew to a height of fifty feet (15m) or more.

Take the left fork to continue the walk. (A path to the right gives the option of visiting a second waterfall.) The ladder stile brings you onto a forest track in a mature and open coniferous woodland of spruce, pine and larch, a peaceful stretch which leads to a gate and onto Barden Fell. There is an abrupt change of view from woodland to the open moor, and the path leads straight on to cross Great Agill Beck, a good grassy spot for a picnic. Rabbits also thought it a good place to establish their warren, which otherwise is totally surrounded by inedible, bracken-covered slopes. The track has been surfaced with limestone chippings, which make a good road for the grouse-shooting parties in August. The higher part of Barden Fell is a heather-covered moorland, interrupted by rock piles such as Truckle Crags, Lord's Seat and Little Simon's Seat.

The heather moors appear to be bleak and there is a sameness of colour and texture that seems to carry on to the horizon, but in August this changes dramatically to a carpet of purple. There are several birds which make it their home. The red grouse stays all year round unless the winter is very hard. A close look at the male grouse in the breeding season reveals a plump, handsome bird, with a vermilion red comb on each side of its head and a much darker colouring than the female.

The male will often stand on a vantage point above the heather. Keep a look out for our smallest falcon, the merlin, which is occasionally seen on Barden Fell as it dashes along close to the heather in pursuit of its prey of meadow pipit, skylark or twite. The smaller male merlin is not much bigger than a blackbird, and does most of the hunting during the breeding season, the nest being deep in the heather. An exciting event is to see the short-eared owl patrolling the moor in broad daylight.

The top of Simon's Seat affords a magnificent panorama of the surrounding country, a surprise view over a steep drop to the Skyreholme Valley below. Grimwith Reservoir can be seen with Fancarl Crag just below it, and Trollers Gill and Parcival Hall below that. More to the left the green reef knolls stand out against Barden Moor with Barden Reservoir. Further to the left and far below lie the scattered, diminutive buildings that make up the village of Skyreholme.

Follow the sign to Howgill, along the edge of the moor, to descend steeply through the wooded hillside towards the river. Below the woods a fine view of of the Wharfe valley may be seen, with Appletreewick on the right and a wooded ridge across the valley just above Howgill. The ridge is now cut through by the river, forming a deep gorge. For a time, towards the end of the Ice Age, the snout of the Wharfe glacier remained stuck at this point and pushed stones, sand and mud into a pile across the valley, damming it completely. This is the Drebley terminal moraine.

The left bank of the river is soon reached by crossing the road and taking the path through the farmyard. The Drebley stepping stones are in good shape and have been well used, the nearest bridge now being that at Barden, over a mile (2km) down river.

Along this mile of riverside there is some good birdwatching, particularly in the spring and summer. The sand martin is the smallest of the three members of the swallow family that visit us, and often arrives by the end of March. They nest in the steep, sandy riverbank, and are joined over the river by swallows as they both feed on the wing, twittering and swooping incessantly over the water. By about the middle of April the brown and white common sandpiper arrives. Its clear, piping notes may be heard as the bird flicks and glides low over the water, its wings in a curved bow. Also to be seen along this stretch, though not always associated with the river, is the reed bunting. The male is outstanding with its white collar and black head, the female being more drably coloured.

Among many outstanding bridges in the Dales, the one at Barden must count as the most beautiful. The large graceful arches that lift the narrow road high over the river and the substantial angular buttresses make it impressive, and it fits so perfectly into its surroundings of woods and fells. The bridge was rebuilt after it was destroyed by a disastrous flood in 1673, when six other bridges over the Wharfe were also washed away. A stone in the bridge is inscribed: 'This bridge was repared at the charge of the whole West Riding, 1676'. New parapets were added in 1856.

On the other side of the river, the dramatic ruin of Barden Tower is full of fascinating history. Replacing a former hunting lodge, it was built by Henry Clifford, the 'Shepherd Lord'. In the Wars of the Roses the young Henry Clifford's father was killed in battle, and the boy was taken by his mother and secretly brought up by shepherds in the Lake District. Twenty-five years later, Lord Clifford returned to build his new residence at Barden, where he lived and studied alchemy and astrology. In 1513, at the age of sixty, he led a troop of men from local villages to victory against the Scots at the battle of Flodden Field in Northumberland. Four generations later, Lady Anne Clifford rebuilt Barden Tower and spent some time there in 1663, only for her descendants to partly dismantle it in the 1770s.

Follow either bank downstream to the fine Victorian battlemented aqueduct, built over the rocky river bed, which brings water from the river Nidd to supplement Bradford's water supply. Then keep to the left bank to enter Strid Wood, designated as a Site of Special Scientific Interest for its plants and birdlife. The riverbed is rocky and narrows as it approaches the Strid. Here there are many round holes in the bedrock, worn by pebbles being swirled round and round in the current. The narrow cleft through which the river flows has been formed by this pot-holing action, and is twenty-five feet (8m) deep and opens out under the water. Several people have been drowned here. The first victim features in the legend of the Boy of Egremond, who was pulled back by his hound when making the jump. It is said that, just before a person drowns in the Strid, a white horse with a foaming mane rises from the swirling waters.

In May the path from the Strid is rich with wild flowers. There are clumps of red campion, glades of wild garlic and miniature forests of bugle. There are bluebells and sweet-smelling woodruff, wild arum and purple wood cranesbill. There are the once-rare peacock butterflies, and plenty of orange tips, green-veined whites and small tortoiseshells. On a quiet morning or evening, you may be lucky enough to see the shy roe deer. In the autumn it replaces its sleek, fox-red summer coat by a grey-brown winter one. Its white rump patch shows up well as it scampers away. There are no grazing sheep along here, so it shoudn't be difficult to identify its cloven hoof prints in muddy places. Further along, tree planting has been carried out to maximise the attraction of wildlife to the area.

Bolton Woods are renowned among ornithologists for the wealth of birdlife to be seen and heard here. A good ear for bird-calls is essential in the spring and early summer, when there is so much cover for the birds. At this time, among the willow warblers, wrens and blackbirds, listen for the trilling song of the woodwarbler or the beautiful clear warbling notes of the blackcap. A rare favourite to look out for in the spring is the pied flycatcher, with its smart black and white plumage as it catches an insect on the wing and settles on a nearby twig with a flick of its wings and tail.

With patience and a good pair of binoculars the list may be added to, and at dusk the woodcock may be seen on its 'roding' flight above the tree tops. If you listen very carefully you may hear its froggy croak and a soft whistle. A short step further and the walk comes its full circle to the wooden bridge and the Cavendish Pavilion.

WALK 3: BARDEN MOOR RESERVOIRS

Start: Halton Height car park. Grid Ref: 038 556
Distance: 5 miles (8km)
OS Maps: Outdoor Leisure 10 or Landranger 104
Walking Time: 3 hours

A fine walk on a sunny day to get the feel of heather moors, to see water birds on the two reservoirs, a gull colony and typical moorland birds and insects. There are excellent views across the valley of Barden Fell and Simon's Seat. Halton Height car park is one mile up the Embsay road from Barden Tower, and makes a good starting point for a very pleasant walk.

Barden Moor is part of the access area of the estate of the Duke of Devonshire, open to the public on most days of the year, though it may be closed for grouse shooting on certain days in late August and during September, or during a period of drought when there is any danger of fire. What appears to be a bleak stretch of peat moorland is full of variety in its scenery and interest. The moors are covered in heather, with a scattering of bilberry, crowberry and bracken, and a few rowan trees grow in sheltered places. This rather special environment is the habitat of several birds and insects that in one way or another depend on the heather for their survival.

From Halton Height car park, take the tarmac track just below the cattle grid which leads down to the lower Barden Reservoir, then left at a crossing of the ways along a track with a view over the water. With binoculars you may be able to make out some of the birds along the margins of the reservoir. Mallard are usually present, numbering up to a hundred, and in winter months there may be sightings of the less common greylag geese, goldeneye or whooper swan, though generally it is the upper reservoir which attracts the most birds.

From the footbridge at the top end of the reservoir you get an impression of the scale of some of the massive Victorian engineer-

ing work carried out here to provide the rapidly growing city of Bradford with an ample water supply. The millstone grit ensures a good surface run-off of soft water, which has been of great value in the woollen industry. The lower reservoir formed part of a major scheme to supply the city with water in the mid-nineteenth century, with a chain of five reservoirs from Grimwith to Bradford. This far-sighted plan was designed and carried out by the chief engineer to Bradford Corporation Waterworks, John Wignall Leather, a relative of mine. Many problems were encountered during the building of the seventy-two foot (22m) high dam and, although it was almost ready in 1863, it was only brought into use ten years later, together with Grimwith, Chelker and Silsden.

The whinchat nests in this area. It is a small migrant and arrives early in April after a long flight from south of the Sahara, an amazing feat for a bird no bigger than a robin. The white stripe over the eye, black face-patches and buff-coloured breast distinguish the male from the female. Both may be seen perching on a tall bracken stem to deliver a brief warbling song. This is the only place in the upper dale where you may come across that rare and beautiful snake, the adder. They are seldom seen but, following hibernation,

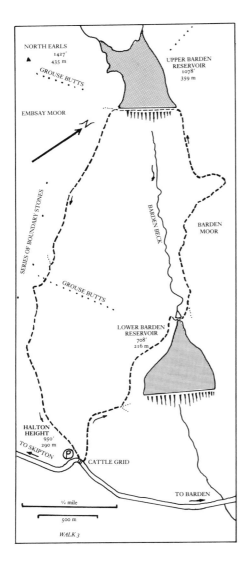

NORTH EARLS
1427'
435 m
GROUSE BUTTS

UPPER BARDEN
RESERVOIR
1078'
359 m

EMBSAY MOOR

SERIES OF BOUNDARY STONES

BARDEN BECK

BARDEN
MOOR

GROUSE BUTTS

LOWER BARDEN
RESERVOIR
708'
216 m

HALTON
HEIGHT
950'
290 m
TO SKIPTON

CATTLE GRID

TO BARDEN

½ mile

500 m

WALK 3

covers the moors and which turns purple in August. The flowers have a sheen on them which is responsible for the glow on the heather when in full bloom. Bell heather, *Erica cinerea*, grows on drier, poor sandy soils so, if you find yourself in boggy ground, make for the tufts of bell heather. Take care to distinguish between bell heather and cross-leaved heath, *Erica tetralix*, which grows in wet places and has clusters of paler pink flowers round the tops of the stems.

Red grouse, which feed almost entirely on the shoots of ling, are always present, either in pairs or in flocks of a dozen or more. Heather is an evergreen, so the grouse remain on the moors all the year round except in the most severe winters, when deep snow may seal off the main food plant. The birds are then driven into the dale where they feed on grasses and rushes. In fact the red grouse is an extremely hardy bird, and in wintery conditions will tread snow for hours to avoid being buried in a snow drift; eggs and chicks can survive spring snow and frosts. The 'keeping' of the heather moors for the shooting parties ensures plenty of heather and therefore good stocks of this uniquely British game bird. Gamekeepers carefully burn off sections of the old heather in narrow strips, which produces more young shoots for the next three or four years. Sheep also graze the heather, and a combination of a moderate number of sheep, along with the resident grouse, is a most efficient use of these marginal lands.

Another creature to feed on the heather is a large, brown woolly caterpillar, the larva of the northern eggar moth. Since the moth has a two year cycle, the caterpillars are common only in even-numbered years! These moors are their ideal habitat, since the males are fast, day-flying insects and require plenty of space to career around in. Its relative the fox moth has a similar

warm themselves in the early spring sunshine. This is our only poisonous snake but is very timid and normally slips away when disturbed.

You can identify the three heathers on this walk. Ling is the other name for the common heather, *Calluna vulgaris*, which

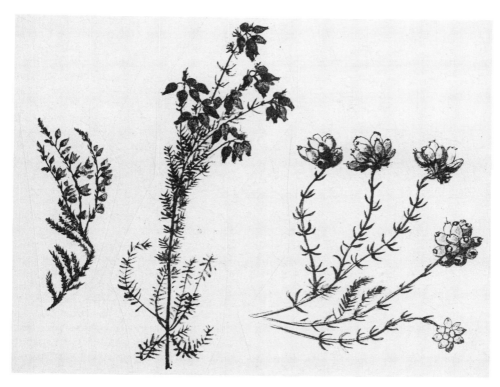

Three heathers (from left to right): common heather or ling, bell heather and cross-leaved heath.

lifestyle, the hairs of the dark brown caterpillar being highly irritant. The moth is a reddish-brown colour with a wingspan of two inches (5cm). Another striking insect to inhabit the heather moors is the even larger emperor moth, with bold eye markings in the middle of each wing. The males again are daytime fliers and the caterpillar is easy to distinguish, being large and bright green with yellow spots.

Two other insects to look for are the seven spot ladybird and the green hairstreak butterfly. Ladybirds hibernate in the leaf debris among the roots of the heather plant and come out to sun themselves in the March sunshine, looking like little red

berries. The green hairstreak is a very small butterfly which looks like a shred of brown paper blowing about, until it lands when it shows the metallic-green upper side of its wings. It then seems to vanish as the tiny wings are indistinguishable from the green leaves of the bilberry, its food plant.

Join the main track from Barden which climbs to the upper reservoir. You will no doubt have seen meadow pipits along the way. Their white outer tail feathers are not so conspicuous, but their habits give them away. In their territorial song-flight they utter a few tuneless notes as they rise up into the air from the heather, and then they parachute down again with wings fluttering

43

and tail up in a more tuneful song. When familiar with them you call them mipits! This is curlew country, and such a large bird – about twenty-two inches (55cm) in length – with its curving bill is easily seen as it planes over its nesting grounds, wings bowed. Its haunting call is unmistakable but it is a wary bird and in retreat its pale rump is distinctive.

Go over the embankment of upper Barden Reservoir for some more bird-watching. A colony of up to 1,000 black-headed gulls breed here each spring. (A smaller colony breeds on Grassington Moor.) The head of this slender gull is actually chocolate brown, and in winter it loses its brown hood altogether. It feeds on moths, caterpillars, beetles, worms and slugs. Lesser black-backed gulls also frequent this reservoir, nesting on the moor above. You may see some common gulls and a few pairs of Canada geese too.

After admiring more work of the Victorian water engineers, take the path signed Halton Height, following a causeway across a bog of rushes and sphagnum moss. This is a peat bog in the making. It is formed where the ground is constantly wet in an area of heavy rainfall – annual rainfall here being fifty inches (1,300mm). There is an absence of oxygen, so the plant debris does not readily decompose and new growth is rooted in the dead vegetation. The soft rush, *Juncus effusus*, which grows here contains a continuous pith. At one time the pith was made use of by repeatedly dipping it in sheep's fat to make rush lights.

The walk continues to provide wonderful views across the fells and over to Simon's Seat on the other side of Wharfedale where the forest plantations merge well into the dale landscape. The plantations have an irregular edge and more than one species has been planted, giving the hillside a variety of colour. You may catch sight of a hare along here. The brown hare is quite able to live in this exposed, open habitat where cold winds and heavy rain are a challenge to its survival. The hare will frequently pop its head up as it looks out for danger, its long, black-tipped ears and larger size differentiating it from the rabbit.

Bear left at each junction in the track to reach the Halton Height car park once more.

WALK 4: APPLETREEWICK AND TROLLERS GILL

Start: Appletreewick. Grid Ref: 053 601
Distance: 5½ miles (9km)
OS Maps: Outdoor Leisure 10 or Landranger 104 and 98
Walking Time: 3 hours

This is an easy walk and takes in a lovely stretch of the river. It then goes on to explore the most geologically interesting limestone area in Wharfedale – Trollers Gill. To reach Appletreewick, turn off the B6160 at Barden Tower. There is limited parking space in the village.

The delightful Dales village of Appletreewick – 'the village by the apple trees' – is spread along a winding hill, with its attractive stone cottages and fascinating buildings, and it boasts three stately halls, a Lord Mayor of London, an ancient annual fair and two pubs. The village was important in early times. The old Monk's Hall was at one time a grange of Bolton Priory. The three to four day 'Aptrick' Fair was held in October in the fields between the village and the river. Sheep, cattle and ponies were brought from far beyond the bounds of Yorkshire. The fair was famous for its onions, known locally as 'winter beef', which were hung along the walls of Onion Lane.

In 1548, Sir William Craven was born here in a small cottage, and as a young man was sent to London to be an apprentice to a draper. He was extremely industrious and when he was fifty became Lord Mayor of London, after which he returned to Appletreewick to build High Hall, which still has its minstrel gallery. His son became a distinguished soldier and married a princess, the sister of Charles I, to become the first Earl of Craven.

The village lies on the edge of the lead-mining area, and several green roads fan north from here to the old mines of Trollers Gill, Dry Gill and Greenhow.

Walk down the road in the direction of Burnsall. Just past the village take the walled lane on the left, then left along the riverside footpath. The flat fields of the river floodplain have been cut through by the Wharfe to a lower level, and downstream the remnants of the old floodplain now form river terraces. If you are not in too much of a hurry you may be rewarded with a flash of turquoise as a kingfisher appears on the scene, the most brilliantly coloured of British birds. Except after a particularly severe winter, a breeding pair may be found every mile or so along the dale. The now fairly common great spotted woodpecker also inhabits this area. The white patches on its short wings are prominent in its swooping flight, or you may hear a drumming as it taps its bill on a dead bough. In the autumn the hips and haws in the extensive bushy area along on the left attract flocks of blackbirds, fieldfares and redwings. The path follows the river into a peaceful wooded gorge, where it has cut not only through the glacial debris of the Drebley moraine but into solid rock beneath to form a deep and narrow channel in the gritstone, deep enough for sub aqua diving.

On reaching the road, turn left for a few paces and cross the stile signed Skyreholme on the right. This brings you onto a ridge with a splendid view. Along the ravine on the right flows Skyreholme Beck, which descends from Trollers Gill. At the farm join the road again, passing through part of

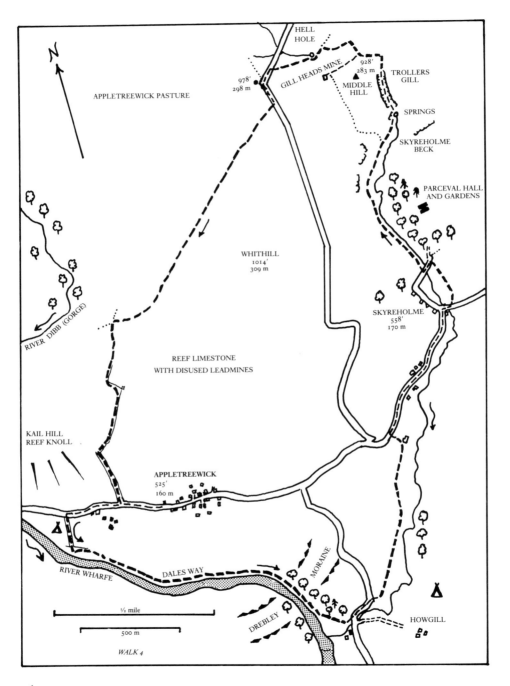

Skyreholme. After a right turn, take the path alongside Skyreholme Beck signed Parceval Hall, or walk up the lane. The hall, said to be the finest residential building in the dale, is dated 1671 and has some lovely gardens which are open to the public in the summer months. The path soon comes out onto the lane again. Turn left over a wooden bridge and follow the sign to Gill Head and New Road up the left side of the beck.

The route passes Skyreholme Dam, which once supplied water for a paper mill in the village. The dam burst in 1899 and was never repaired. On approaching Trollers Gill, avoid the path up the hill to the left and keep straight on. A rocky bank on the left is spectacular in the spring when it is dotted with the pink flowers of doves-foot cranesbill. In the early summer, rockroses and hawkweeds grow here. The brilliant yellow rockrose, no relation of the rose, has the most delicate and thin petals, but, though insects visit it for its pollen, it has no scent or nectar.

A little further on, springs of clear water gush out of the ground where wild water-cress grows. There must be some imper-meable rock not far below the surface which forces the springs to break out here. The rocks beneath the limestone may be Silurian slate, a similar situation to the springs at Kilnsey Crag. Across on the right from this point there are fine screes below Nape Scar, on which a few yew trees cling, and the view up the branching valley clearly shows the bending over of the strata at the core of the Skyreholme anticline. Cross the stile to enter Trollers Gill — or Jackdaw Nick as it is also called — but turn back if you are superstitious or if you have a wild imagination. The trolls roll rocks down from overhead and the barguest, the spectre hound of Craven, has a cave in the gill. Once a cobbler from Thorpe lost his way here and saw the huge shaggy beast:

'Yellow, wi' such eyes! They war as big as saucers. This mun be a barguest, thowt I, an' counted mesel fer dead!'.

Trollers Gill is a superb miniature gorge cut through the Great Scar limestone, 300 yards long and just a few yards across. Over the stile there is a cliff on the left where some interesting plants hang on to ledges. At its foot grows mossy saxifrage with its creeping mossy leaves and attractive white flowers, a plant that likes rocks and screes and a non acid soil. Higher up the gill you can compare shining cranesbill and herb robert with the dovesfoot cranesbill of lower down.

After a heavy downpour of rain I have seen the gorge awash with rushing brown water filling its whole width, but most of the time it is dry. The work of water erosion is to be seen in the undercutting of the lime-stone in the side of the gorge. High on the

The entrance to Trollers Gill.

right there are one or two adits for lead, and white lumps of calcite can be found in the stream bed, a mineral which can be broken into a perfect rhombohedron (a shape like a cube knocked sideways). In winter you may find the skillfully-eaten carcasses of rabbits in the gill, a sure sign of the presence of stoats in the area. The skin is turned back and the good fleshy parts eaten to the bone, leaving a neat bag of entrails. The stoat is a fierce hunter and can kill prey twice its own size. It may sometimes be seen upright and looking about, revealing its creamy underside. At the iron bar, climb up to the left and over the stile to join the track to examine Gill Head Mine down to the left.

The mine is now closed and the machinery has been removed, but in the 1970s two local prospectors worked the mine for fluorite and sold it to the steel industry. The fluorite came from one large 'pocket' at the side of the vein. The line of the vein can be followed on the hillside above the mine, as well as on the slopes opposite, and is roughly parallel to the Craven Fault. Among the bits of fluorite, which have a dirty, watery appearance, look for the square edges of cubic crystals – some pure pieces show the faint purple colour of Blue John along the crystal margins.

You may also find bits of galena, the ore of lead, a bright silvery-grey when freshly broken. It is thought that the mine produced large tonnages of the precious ore in the past. Little grows on the tip heaps because of the poisonous presence of lead, except for the tiny white flowers of spring sandwort, which is so common near such old mines it is said to be an indicator of lead.

Retreat up the mine track to where it turns sharp right, and at this point leave the track and keep straight on to visit Hell Hole. It is here that a small stream, after flowing over shales, disappears down an impressive sink in the Great Scar lime-

stone. The pothole is 100 feet (30m) deep, and at the entrance the surface of the limestone is full of rounded nodules – calcareous algae by the name of *Girvanella*. This rock layer is a marker bed known as the Girvanella Band, which separates the Great Scar limestone from the Yoredale series above.

Follow the stream upwards and bear left to the ladder stile, and over the wall to the road. Go left for 220 yards (200m) to where the track starts across the moor signed 'Hartlington'. On the left is the old mine railway track from Gill Head Mine. The rails have been removed, except for two short tell-tale stumps embedded in the edge of the road.

In spring and early summer, on the limestone pasture leading back to Appletreewick, you may see the broad white wingbars of the redshank in its rather erratic flight,

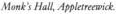

Monk's Hall, Appletreewick.

48

adding its loud scolding call. Another bird which gives itself away by the sound it makes during its aerial display is the smaller wader, the snipe. Not a song this, but a drumming created by air vibrating its tail feathers as it glides sharply downward with tail outspread.

The newly built-up track eventually turns into a green lane, and at the crossroad of footpaths take the left one to Appletree-wick. From this winding farm track, five of the reef knolls can be seen, with the large rounded Kail Hill in the foreground, a hill with a former Iron Age camp on the top and lots of small lead workings on its side. The winding track becomes walled, and narrows and steepens as it ends at the village stocks by the Craven Arms.

WALK 5: GRIMWITH RESERVOIR

Start: Grimwith Reservoir car park. Grid Ref: 063 640
Distance: 4½ miles (7km)
OS Maps: Outdoor Leisure 10 or Landranger 98
Walking Time: 2 to 2½ hours

This is essentially a birdwatcher's stroll in a modern landscape – the new reservoir was opened in 1985. Turn off the B6265, the Grassington to Pateley Bridge road, near the brow of the hill above Dibble's Bridge. At the end of a new road are the car park and toilets provided by Yorkshire Water. There is a charge for parking at Grimwith.

The embankment replaces the old Victorian dam, now hidden in the base of the new one. Situated nearly 1,000 feet (300m) above sea level, the new dam is 130 feet (40m) high and over 1,100 yards (1km) long, and the reservoir is the biggest expanse of inland water in Yorkshire. Here is not only a new landscape and a new environment, but a new habitat. It is attracting an associated wildlife and, as a large inland freshwater lake with developing mudflats, Grimwith is known as an important sanctuary for certain waders, ducks and geese. Around the reservoir is an extensive area of rough grassland and bracken, which in the spring and summer also harbours a rich birdlife. Beyond this the land rises to heather moors.

The building of the new dam was a major engineering achievement. To start with, there were several geological problems to be overcome. There were a few old bell pits to a coal seam in the Grassington grit, the vertical shafts of which had to be filled in and sealed. The strata in the vicinity of the dam dip at an angle of eight degrees, and include a bed of shales between ones of limestone and sandstone. The shales were likely to become saturated with water, making them liable to slip. In order to avoid this, high-tension steel wires were passed through the three rock layers, anchoring the shale securely. Vertical drainage holes were also made through the shales into the limestone below, which acted as a soakaway. Before the dam could be started, the River Dibb had to be diverted through a 200 yard (185m) long tunnel.

The embankment took ten years of hard work to build, with the movement of 3,000,000 tons of material. The glacial clay and shale of which it is constructed came from the western end of the reservoir basin. Placed and rolled in layers, it incorporates the old dam in its upstream shoulder. Drainage layers in the dam and the upstream face are made of crushed gritstone from a quarry on the east side of the reservoir. This has been smoothed and landscaped, and now provides an access for vehicles and boats.

From the car park, make for the dam and walk along the top of the embankment. An early start on a calm day is best, and a quiet approach is essential if you want to avoid the tantalising scene of many of the shore birds making off onto the middle of the lake and out of range of easy identification. The combined valve tower and overflow is an imposing edifice, with the depth of water marked in metres on the side of the tower. Down to the left by the control house, the

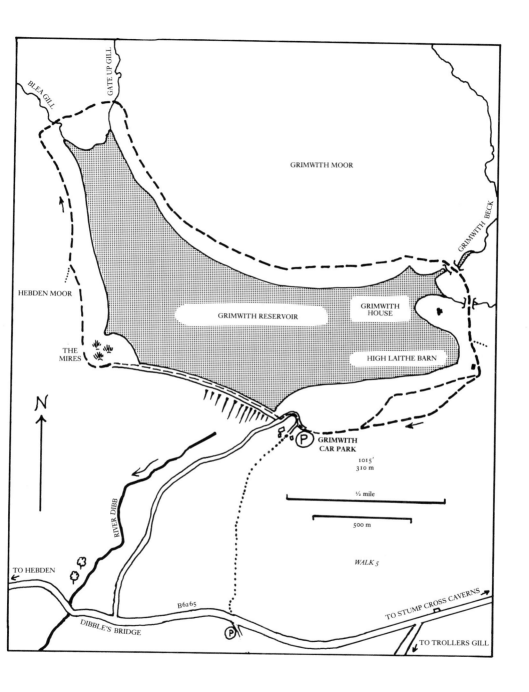

BLEA GILL

GATE UP GILL

GRIMWITH MOOR

GRIMWITH BECK

HEBDEN MOOR

GRIMWITH RESERVOIR

GRIMWITH HOUSE

THE MIRES

HIGH LAITHE BARN

N

GRIMWITH CAR PARK

1015'
310 m

½ mile

500 m

RIVER DIBB

WALK 5

TO HEBDEN

TO STUMP CROSS CAVERNS

B6265

DIBBLE'S BRIDGE

TO TROLLERS GILL

outlet tunnel is capable of taking 500,000 cubic feet (200m³) of water per second from the overflow shaft.

The ringed plover normally breeds along our coasts – but there they face disturbance to their habitat. So many of these birds go miles inland to breed by quieter and less-frequented lakes and rivers. In summer, ringed plover and their chicks may be seen from the dam. Grimwith is their only breeding place in Wharfedale. They can be distinguished from their rarer relative, the little ringed plover, by the pale wing-bar, heavier build, and in adults, orange-yellow legs. Further along, redshanks, dunlin and oystercatchers feed in the mud and on the grassy banks. On the water there are likely to be large numbers of Canada geese, perhaps a hundred or more, again with young, in June and July. Heron, too, should not be difficult to spot.

At the end of the dam the path turns north and keeps a useful distance above the shore, though care must still be taken not to disturb the water birds and send them scattering. There are quite a few patches of thistles around the reservoir, which attract a large number of insects and birds. In July, small colonies of small tortoiseshell butterflies flit about on the old thistle heads, and parties of twite may be seen feeding on the thistle seeds. In fact, thistles are rather like oak trees in the way they attract a rich insect life. There are three common thistles. The one with the large, purple flower head is the spear thistle. Creeping thistle has slimmer flower heads, and reproduces by a creeping root system as well as its thistle down. Marsh thistle has small flower heads, which can be shades of purple or even white, and the leaves are usually tinged with purple.

Hartlington Moor Lane comes in from the left, and around the buildings here pied wagtails and starlings are in evidence. This northern end of Grimwith Reservoir has the greatest concentration of birds. Many moorland birds are to be seen along here too. The lapwing is common, and you may see it in spring, tumbling in an aerial display over its territory as it rolls and twists in a seemingly uncontrolled earthward plunge. The wild call of the curlew is a wonderful sound in the early part of the year. It is Europe's biggest wader and is easily recognised by its long, downward-curving bill. While the eggs are being incubated the curlew is quiet, but when the eggs are hatched the parents become much more noisy and aggressive, sometimes swooping on intruders.

Breeding ducks to see in the spring and summer include mallard, tufted duck and, if you are lucky, teal, our smallest native duck. The handsome teal drake has a 'crick, crick' call and the duck a sharp high-pitched quack. Grimwith is now one of the few places outside Scotland where wigeon breed and the reservoir is becoming a nationally important site for them. In 1989 eleven pairs bred here. The drake gives a piping 'whee-oo' whistling call which can be heard from a distance. Wigeon are also present in winter, when they are joined by goosander and goldeneye. The latter is a true winter visitor, the drake having striking black and white plumage with a white spot on the side of its black face. They are great divers and can travel some distance under water.

On the edge of the moor look out for the short-eared owl. When perched on a rock or post it can be distinguished from other owls by its more horizontal attitude. In the breeding season it is easier to see than most other owls, as it hunts by day. Its favourite food is the field vole, a fast breeder that can lead to a population explosion. The vole is

Goldeneye.

The rebuilt High Laithe cruck barn.

four inches (10cm) long, has yellowy-brown fur and a short tail. This grass-eating rodent likes to live in tussocks of grass, bilberry or heather. Ring ouzels may be seen near the first bridge over Blea Gill, overlooked by rocky crags. The stream comes down from Blea Gill Water-fall and through the narrow gorge below it. Cross Gate Up Gill and along the edge of Grimwith Moor, and further on you may see the white rump of the wheatear and its relative the whinchat.

Pass Grimwith House and the footpath which branches off to Stump Cross Cavern (a mile away over the moor), then High Laithe barn. This is a rebuilt 'raised cruck' barn with a steep ling-thatched roof, a reminder of how barns may have looked in the fifteenth and sixteenth century. Take either path back to the car park.

WALK 6: BURNSALL TO THORPE

Start: Burnsall. Grid Ref: 032 612
Distance: 4½ miles (7km)
OS Maps: Outdoor Leisure 10 or Landranger 98
Walking Time: 2½ hours

This must be the most beautiful short walk in Wharfedale and it makes a perfect family outing. Beginning at the delightfully situated village of Burnsall, it takes in a favourite stretch of river, a wander through green limestone knolls to the hidden hamlet of Thorpe, then returns through the fields.

The best approach to Burnsall is up the dale from Bolton Abbey, when suddenly from the top of the hill the village comes into view. It is an arresting and picturesque scene, dominated by the fine bridge of five arches over the wide river. The attractive sixteenth century tower of the little church rises behind a cluster of stone roofs and buildings set among the green slopes and hills in the heart of the dale. The village looks south down the dale, and the view from Burnsall itself is also striking, with a wide sweep of the river in the foreground and the green rounded Kail Hill on the left. This contrasts with the dark and steep mass of Burnsall Fell on the right.

The church is well worth a visit, being one of the most outstanding in the Dales. Founded by St Wilfred in about AD 690, the oldest parts date from 1150. It has been restored several times and on one occasion, in 1612, restoration was paid for by Sir William Craven. In the church are the remains of four eleventh century crosses bearing Anglian and Danish designs, and also a remarkable font with Danish markings. Early burials were covered by stone, hog-backed grave lids, like a tiled roof with a beast carved at each end. The best of these is now in Skipton Museum. A beautiful alabaster carving of the Nativity is possibly fifteenth century and is mounted in the north-east chapel. The attractive ancient lych-gate swings on an unusual

centre post and is thought to be the only one of its kind in Yorkshire. The village stocks are situated in the churchyard. Below the church, the very fine Elizabethan building is the grammar school, founded by Sir William Craven in 1603. It is a beautiful old building with mullioned windows and large porch. Almost unchanged, it is still in use as a first school for local children.

The old grammar school at Burnsall.

Burnsall is noted for its traditional sports and fell race which take place on the third Saturday in August, close to the feast day of St Wilfred. The race is to the top of Burnsall Fell and back, which the best runners can do in under fifteen minutes.

Start the walk by going to the right of the Red Lion and along the river path to Loup Scar. The river here runs in an enchanting narrow gorge and tall majestic trees above the steep sides emphasise its depth. Rookeries occupy the biggest of the trees. The first limestone crag across the river is Wilfred Scar – named perhaps because St Wilfred baptised new believers here. Loup Scar is a second and more imposing vertical limestone cliff, rising high above the river where a close look shows some of the strata to be strongly folded, indicating that we are still south of the Craven Fault. In the spring there is a wealth of wild flowers and the beautiful, white meadow saxifrage grows by the path opposite Loup Scar. This is a plant that favours well-drained calcareous soils. Each stem branches into several flower heads, the five white petals having green veins.

The well-maintained footpath leads to Hebden via the suspension bridge. There are lots of flowers growing along this part of the walk. Among them is lady's mantle, a small inconspicuous plant with a greenish-yellow flower whose pleated leaves collect large pearly drops of dew. Alchemists thought the dew had special properties so they collected it at dawn. It was used in their experiments to make gold from base metals, hence the flower's Latin name of *Alchemilla vulgaris*. Another undistinguished plant is salad burnet, the leaves of which may be used in salads. The rounded flower head has male flowers on the lower part which come out first, rich with yellow pollen. The female flowers higher up open later, thus preventing these wind-pollinated plants being self fertilised. An old name for it is cucumber burnet and if you break a leaf you can smell the cucumber.

You may see long-tailed tits in the smaller trees and bushes, or hear the great spotted woodpecker drumming out a message on the branch of a dead elm. The river is the haunt of the brilliantly-coloured yellow wagtail, and you may see pied and grey wagtails too. Of the three it is the grey wagtail that is truly a river bird. You will soon come to the suspension bridge which replaced old and worn stepping stones, the remains of which are still to be seen in the river. The bridge is now getting old and is to be repaired.

Lady's mantle.

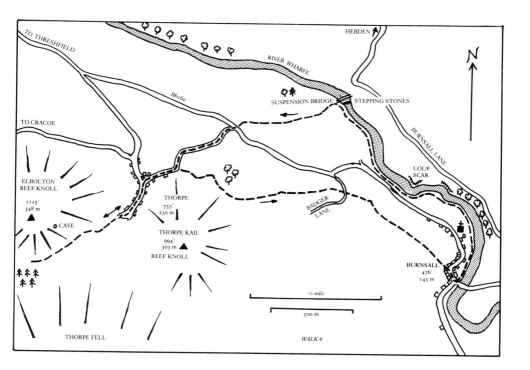

Instead of crossing the bridge, take the path to the left, up the bank away from the river and signposted 'Bridleway to Thorpe'. This leads to the road through the fields, with an ever-improving view of the surrounding countryside. In the autumn, wild mushrooms dot the fields. They have much more flavour than the cultivated varieties. Cross the road and take the small, winding road opposite, which soon brings you to the hidden and fascinating village of Thorpe.

The Danish meaning of 'outlying hamlet' is a good description, for there is no shop, chapel or pub here. In fact 'Thorpe-in-the-hollow' is mainly a collection of working farms, a manor house, and miscellaneous houses and cottages. The buildings themselves hold much of interest, as some

of the tiny old cottages are quite unaltered except for being used as barns or farm stores. There are barns of different periods, one with a very fine corbelled porch, and, in the gable of a barn dated 1793, a carved stone face still keeps out the evil spirits. Many of the old cottages must have been occupied by the shoemakers, who for centuries made Thorpe famous for its high-quality footwear: shoes and slippers for the monks of Fountains Abbey, clogs for the lead miners from Grassington and boots for the farming folk. The cobblers travelled miles along the old packhorse routes, carrying new and repaired shoes and returning with others which needed attention. At one time there were as many as forty employed in this cottage industry. It is said if you listen carefully you can still hear the tap-tap-tapping of the merry cobblers of Thorpe.

Stroll past the village green, now replanted with some new young trees, and on to Thorpe Lane which leads out to the sheep pastures on the side of Elbolton. All the roads out of Thorpe go uphill from the village, which lies well sheltered from strong winds between the two limestone knolls of Kail and Elbolton. To the south, Thorpe Fell rises to heather moors. At the end of the walled lane is the remains of an old leadmine. The spoil heap, now grassed over, becomes a purple mass of wild thyme in the summer, with the small yellow dots of black medick and a few carline thistles.

Continue up the path to the brow of the hill near a small conifer plantation. From here, you get a broad view of the grit moors of Thorpe Fell and the green reef knolls of Butter Haw and Stebden. On a summer's day it is a lovely, peaceful place. You may hear the drumming of a snipe as it side-slips through the air, or see the wheatear restlessly hopping about.

Elbolton is the most interesting of the reef knolls of Craven and its pure limestone contains a wonderful variety of well preserved-fossils. It is possible to find a few bits and pieces in the screes and debris thrown out of rabbit holes (but note that hammers are not allowed). This is a specially interesting geological site. Some 330 million years ago, marine life was abundant here, and varied according to the depth of water down the steep sides of the reef. A large proportion consists of types of brachiopod (lampshells); bivalves are also common. There are coiled gonia-tites and straight-coned nautiloids, gastro-pods (snails) and occasional trilobites. There are also crinoid remains (sea-lilies) and corals, algae and sponges, and bryozoans that look like delicate pieces of lace.

As well as being riddled with the shafts and passages of many old mines, Elbolton contains some natural caves. On one side is Knave Knoll Hole, a cave with a twenty foot (6m) vertical shaft which opens out into two passages. In 1889, important finds were made of simple Neolithic pottery, hearths and human skeletons in the crouched position of burial. Footholds were present, worn and polished by years of use where prehistoric people had climbed in and out. Beneath the human remains were the even older bones of grizzly bear and brown bear.

There were always a few believers in the little folk, and Elbolton Hill is traditionally a place for fairies. They danced on the side of the hill in the moonlight, had no objection to onlookers, but if invited to dance you had to join in, otherwise some slight mis-chief may have befallen you.

Retrace your steps to the green lane, through Thorpe and up the road to the right at the lower end of the village. At the top of the rise where a sign points to Burnsall, turn right along a walled lane which leads through the fields back to the village. At the lane end is a familiar National Park ladder stile. On the way there are some superb lynchets along the hillside, as clearly cut as they must have been 700 years ago. Cross Badger Lane. The word badger here is an old dialect word meaning a pedlar or a man who trades in corn. Badger Lane would have been the traditional route of the badger and his pack ponies. Note the ash trees dotted about this limestone landscape and the splendid view ahead. Now negotiate another fourteen stiles or gates to return to the start!

WALK 7: HEBDEN AND YARNBURY

Start: Hebden. Grid Ref: 026 631
Distance: 5½ miles (9km)
OS Maps: Outdoor Leisure 10 or Landranger 98
Walking Time: 3 hours

This is a fascinating walk which concentrates on the old leadmining industry, with a look at a magnificent Bronze Age henge. The going is easy and takes you up the valley of Hebden Gill and onto Grassington Moor. Hebden is on the B6265 near Grassington. There is limited parking space in Hebden village.

The area of Hebden Gill and Grassington Moor is the most intensively mined part of Wharfedale. There are signs of leadmining everywhere: spoil tips litter the landscape, portals to horizontal levels are found in the valley sides and dangerous vertical shafts dot the moor. The industry was at its peak 150 years ago when a large proportion of the male population worked as miners. No lead has been mined for over 100 years, and little remains today of former crushing mills, smelting furnaces, water wheels, diverted streams, dams and miners' cottages. We can only imagine the maze of underground levels, sub-levels, crosscuts and shafts, driven at great human cost to tap the richest veins of the valuable ore.

The village of Hebden overlooks Hebden Beck. It has some old houses, but most of the buildings, including miners' homes, date from the nineteenth century. The church was built in 1841, which saved inhabitants a long walk and a river crossing by stepping stones to attend Linton parish church. Hebden lies on a bus route on the Pateley Bridge road. It has toilets, a village shop and post office, and several well-placed seats from which to admire the surroundings. Apart from its mining relics, Hebden Gill is a pleasant little valley with a variety of habitats for birds and flowers.

The walk begins in the village and crosses the main road. Go over the small stone bridge to the path in front of the cottages to follow the right side of Hebden Gill. This is a beautiful miniature dale, dotted with ash, hawthorn and sycamore, with the waters of Hebden Beck hurrying down among the boulders. In spring the beckside is a mass of scurvygrass and sweet cicely, with kingcups and a scattering of yellow Welsh poppies. Scurvygrass has white flowers with heart-shaped fleshy leaves which contain a high amount of vitamin C, and is generally regarded as a plant of the seaside. Sweet cicely is a large leafy umbellifer (of the carrot family) with white flowers which smell strongly of aniseed. Cross the footbridge to continue along the lane on the other side. Part way along is a glimpse of a pretty waterfall known as Scala Force.

At Hole Bottom take the right fork, following a bridleway over a small stone bridge, keeping to Hebden Gill. Just below the bridge on the far bank is a most interesting botanical site, for growing here are three plants typical of leadmine tip heaps. They tolerate a small amount of lead in their diet. None is impressive, but a close look will reveal spring sandwort, a delicate little white flower growing from a mossy cushion of leaves, alpine pennycress, with a head of small white flowers, growing to about four inches (10cm) from a rosette of

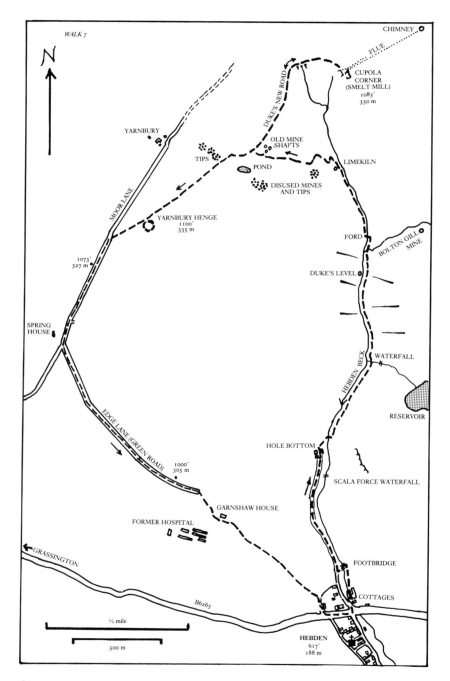

leaves, and the third one is common sorrel, the leaves of which turn bright red in the late summer.

The track passes signs of water engineering, mine tunnel entrances, spoil heaps, ruined mine buildings and a little waterfall then opens out to become a treeless valley. Hebden Gill became the site for the Duke's Level, which was started in 1792. This was a big undertaking to drain water at depth from under the mines of Yarnbury and Grassington Moor. It took thirty years to complete but was successful in allowing an increased depth to be mined. Before the Duke's Level was completed, water had been a serious problem because mines could only go as deep as it was practical to pump water out. The entrance to the Duke's Level, now blocked with a stone wall, can be seen to the left of the beck.

Although there may have been some earlier mining in Hebden Gill, it was passed over by the Dukes of Devonshire when they developed the mines on Grassington Moor. It was not until 1853 that the Hebden Moor Mining Company explored several veins and built modern dressing floors in Hebden Gill, where water was used to separate ore from rock. In Bolton Gill a 210 foot (64m) deep shaft was sunk to a vein known as Bottle Level; tunnels up to 600 yards (570m) were driven from the base of the shaft. The restored arched entrance of this mine can be seen up to the right, from where Bolton Gill meets Hebden Beck. The mine was equipped with pumps and winding gear, powered by a huge waterwheel. A small smelt mill went into operation at Hole Bottom. Over a ten year period from 1855, production was about 300 tons per year, but by 1870 had fallen to only 40 tons; two years later, mining in Hebden Gill ceased altogether. The leadminers were poorly off, earned only a few pence a day and many walked several miles to and from work. They wore clogs with footless stockings, woollen breeches and a leather coat with a pointed tail at the back to shed the water in the dripping tunnels. Thick felt hats took the place of safety helmets and tallow dip candles gave the only light.

The site of the 'crushing floor' at Hebden Gill.

Keep on up the left side of the beck and after the limekiln follow the zigzag track out of the valley. Turn right through a gate and look here for examples of the mineral galena, the lead ore for which the miners worked so hard and risked their lives. Galena is a dull grey colour and it is found with with pale, buff-coloured fluorite. Heft the pieces in your hand until you find one that is much denser than the rest, then smash it open with a large stone. The galena sparkles like silver when freshly broken. It is a sulphide of lead and its chemical formula is PbS, but it also contains a small percentage of silver.

Pass large spoil heaps and a disused mining area on the left to meet up with Dukes New Road at a t-junction. The walk will continue left, but first take a short excursion to the right to Cupola Corner.

Cross the wall by the ladder stile, then go over the dam. This was built across Hebden Beck to hold back a reservoir which is now drained. Negotiate a second ladder stile to reach the site of Cupola smelt mill. The whole of the mining area is now posted with information plaques which explain the different relics and processes: 'The smelt mill', we are told, 'was built in 1793 by the Duke of Devonshire, replacing the original peat and wood burning smelt mill. Fired by coal from local mines this new reverberatory furnace ran continuously and required a high input of ore to make it economical.' One can imagine the hard-working miners exhausting themselves in the effort to produce enough ore to keep the furnace going.

The flue and smelt mill chimney on Grassington Moor.

The ore was heated in an oval hearth, with a good blast of air to get it hot enough to drive off the sulphur fumes. Remember the ore is lead sulphide. All that is needed is heat to give off the sulphur and pure lead metal is left. In the process of smelting, lead was lost to the atmosphere along with the sulphur fumes. So here at Cupola, two flues 600 yards (550m) long were built up the slope of the moor from the smelt mill, and the lead condensed on the inner surface of them like soot, later to be washed or scraped off by small boys who could crawl inside. These flues ended in two tall chimneys, one of which remains today and has recently been restored. It is forty feet (12m) high and is visible for miles around. You can inspect the flues just above the smelt mill. The Grassington Moor mines were producing ore from about the year 1600. By 1760 the annual total was 600 tons, which reached a peak in 1853 with over 2,000 tons of ore. The mines ceased production in 1886, mainly because of competition from cheap imported ores, which resulted in unemployment and poverty.

Return along Dukes New Road to Beever Dam, the small reservoir on the left. The track bears right and the large tip-heaps of Yarnbury mines come into view. Just after Beever Dam and before the first tip, turn left. You can see the route by noting a series of stiles and a gate, one behind the other, across the fields. The first field has outcrops of grit, but the next ones have limestone at the surface and as a result the pastures are better and greener. After squeezing through the fourth stile (in the traditional design of the drystone wall-builders), look on the left for the remarkably well-preserved henge, probably of late Neolithic age. Because it is not a stone henge it is presumed that timber was used in its construction, and is therefore referred to as a woodhenge. It measures 100 feet

Craven of Appletreewick, Richard Fountaine was yet another Dalesman to make his fortune in London and leave some of his wealth to local good works. Having recovered from the plague of 1665, he made a good living from burying the wealthy who did not survive. He helped rebuild the city after the Great Fire of 1666, and later became an alderman of the City of London.

Cross one of the bridges and leave Linton along the left bank of the beck to head for Threshfield, the footpath being the shortest route between the two villages. The path leads down the old lane round Linton House. It crosses some fields to a hump-backed footbridge over the former railway line, which here lay in a shallow cutting. The Yorkshire Dales railway from Skipton to Grassington was completed in 1902, and was part of a plan to take it under Great Whernside and on into Coverdale as part of a route to Darlington. However, the expense was too great to take it further and, with the advent of the motor car, the line to Grassington closed to passenger traffic in 1929. Part of it is still used by the limestone quarry at Cracoe.

From the footbridge, keep straight on by the wall, then at the next field strike diagonally across it to reach Threshfield. Turn right over Threshfield Bridge, the enormous top stones of which are covered in the fleshy leaves of biting stonecrop or wallpepper, a mass of yellow in the summer. Across the road is the Old Hall Inn, behind which there are some of the oldest domestic buildings in Wharfedale, including part of the Old Hall. The ancient mullioned windows are the same shape as those of the gatehouse of the monastic grange at Kilnsey, and the building could possibly date from as early as the fourteenth century. Other buildings across the green are dated 1625 and 1640, and an old barn had small living quarters for a cow hand or hind, who would look after the cattle below.

Threshfield used to be famous for its besoms, brooms made from twigs of heather gathered from the moors and tied neatly with strips of wood to a stout stick of hazel or ash. The besom-makers would go round the dale, selling them for a few pence each. Like Grassington, the village has expanded in modern times and has quite a few twentieth century houses, many being the homes of people who work in Leeds or Bradford.

Go along the road opposite the pub and past the parish noticeboard to reach the road from Bolton Abbey. Turn right for 60 yards (55m) and take the second field path, marked 'Public bridleway to Threshfield School', along an old lynchet to another footbridge over the non-existent railway to the school. A tercentenary tablet on the building says: 'Founded in 1674 by the Rev Matthew Hewitt rector of the ancient parish of Linton'. Once a grammar school, whose pupils included Dr T D Whitaker, the historian of Craven, the buildings are still in use as Threshfield Primary School. They are said to be haunted by the gentle ghost of Old Pam the Fiddler. Pam was a master of the school who was known the length of the dale for his fiddle playing. One night the parish rector, who did not take kindly to the music, found Pam playing his fiddle and snatched it from him. A fight started and poor old Pam died in the struggle. If you pass the school at night and peep in, you may see his ghost quietly playing.

Turn left, and in just under 200 yards take the river path to Linton Falls. Cross the former mill stream by Li'le Emily's Bridge, so named by the local writer, Halliwell Sutcliffe, after Emily Norton, who is said to have crossed it to the sanctuary of the miller's house. The lands of the wealthy, Catholic Norton family, including those of Linton and Threshfield, were confiscated by the Crown for sup-

Linton Falls.

porting the Rising of the North in 1569 and many of the Nortons fled or were beheaded, though Emily found refuge with sympathisers. The story is told in Wordsworth's *White Doe of Rylstone*. The white doe used to be seen on Emily's grave at Bolton Abbey. The bridge is possibly fourteenth century.

A left turn brings you to the splendid 'falls of the Wharfe' and the beautifully-built new wooden footbridge which gives a good overhead view of the river here as it plunges through the limestone. Linton Falls marks the line of the Craven Fault,

with Great Scar limestone upstream and Bowland shales to the south. The soft black shales are clearly visible in the riverbank a little way downstream, opposite Linton church. The tough white limestone has resisted erosion and so a step occurs in the riverbed. The weirs provided water power for the big old textile mill. This has now been replaced by new housing, and the new community of Linton Falls. The two weirs and the waterfall have a total drop of thirty feet (9m). The car park is a few yards further on along the road.

WALK 9: GRASS WOOD FROM GRASSINGTON

Start: Grassington, National Park Centre. Grid Ref: 002 638
Distance: 4½ miles (7km)
OS Maps: Outdoor Leisure 10 or Landranger 98
Walking Time: 2½ hours

This beautiful short walk combines an outstanding part of the river with the delightful and flowery Grass Wood. It is an excellent walk for wild flowers, and for both river and woodland birds. It makes a good family walk. The biggest car park is at the National Park Centre, for which there is a charge.

Grassington is the busiest and most popular centre for Upper Wharfedale, and a very good starting point for walks in all directions. In the heart of the village is the cobbled square, often crowded with people and cars. There are two narrow streets leading from the top of the square, and many interesting corners and 'folds' on each side. The village received its market status in 1282 but really grew in importance during the leadmining period of the eighteenth and early nineteenth centuries, when it prospered and the population increased. A familiar character was Tom Airey, the well-loved postmaster of Grassington, who carried the mail in a horse and trap from Skipton up to Buckden. Tom also ran the Grassington Theatre which his father had founded, and which was widely acclaimed for its Shakespeare and other plays. Tom Airey died in 1842.

Grassington is now the main tourist centre for the dale and has a National Park Information Centre, sectional headquarters and a large car park. There are good shops, many fascinating old buildings and the Upper Wharfedale Museum is well worth a visit. Throughout the year many events take place here, from art exhibitions to Dickensian days.

The walk starts from the National Park Centre. Go through the car park to a gate at the bottom corner which brings you onto the Snake, a narrow walled path down to the river and Linton Falls. This is an interesting approach to the river, as the two weirs which come into view – in addition to the falls themselves – give a clear impression of the drop in the riverbed over a short distance as it passes over the Craven Fault. The new wooden footbridge built in 1989 affords a good view both upstream and down, and of the rushing waters of the Wharfe as they pour over the limestone. It is the dipper that likes the rushing waters of the weir, and the sandpiper may not be far away below the falls.

Take the path up the right side of the Wharfe signed 'To Grass Wood along Riverside'. On the other bank is a disused red brick and concrete building which once provided Grassington with hydro-electricity. Between here and Grassington Bridge, if you haven't spotted either of them already, you may see the white-breasted dipper in whirring straight flight, or the barred wings of the common sandpiper in contrasting jerky flight, with brief glides. Both like fast-running water with plenty of rocks and stones, though you will only see the sandpiper from April to September. Grassington Bridge is one of the oldest across the Wharfe. Built in 1603 to replace a wooden one, it was widened in 1780 and 1984. The downstream section shows the original arches.

At the bridge, cross the road and follow the sign to 'Grass Wood Lane'. The path

69

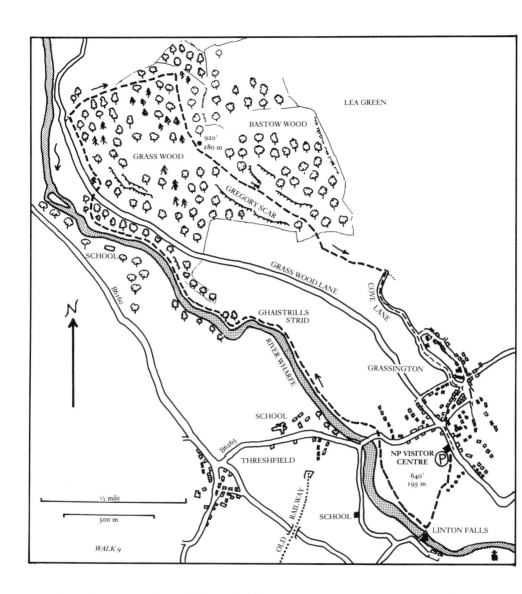

LEA GREEN

BASTOW WOOD

920'
280 m

GRASS WOOD

GREGORY SCAR

SCHOOL

GRASS WOOD LANE

COVE LANE

B6160

N

GHAISTRILLS
STRID

RIVER WHARFE

GRASSINGTON

SCHOOL

NP VISITOR
CENTRE

P

B6265

THRESHFIELD

640'
195 m

½ mile

500 m

OLD RAILWAY

SCHOOL

LINTON FALLS

WALK 9

continues along a most beautiful stretch of the river for another mile and a half (2½ km). This is a great place for birds and flowers. There are several outcrops of Great Scar limestone and then the banks become wooded. At a small footbridge a wet patch includes scurvygrass, a plant that has small white flowers and heart-shaped leaves, and is more common on the coast than inland. The plant is rich in vitamin C and was a cure for scurvy, which used to plague sailors on long sea voyages. The

Scurvygrass.

heavily-scented meadowsweet is another plant of damp places and flowers in July. In centuries past the flowers have been used as an air freshener by scattering them on the farmhouse floor, and also to give flavour to mead.

The river narrows and rushes through the limestone at Ghaistrill's Strid, once avoided by local people as a place of ghosts. The beautiful burnet rose grows here, with its creamy white flowers, very spiny stems and purplish-black hips. It has a special fragrance and grows by the sea as well as in mountainous areas. The rocks are bright with flowers in the spring and early summer, and include the striking bloody cranesbill, a limestone species with large, deep magenta flowers. As for the river here, the walker may wonder why it continues to flow on the surface rather than find an underground route through the limestone. This is because the water table stays at river level – which is fortunate, otherwise the river bed could become dry from time to

time, like that in Langstrothdale and Littondale.

On entering the lovely woodland of Lower Grass Wood, which is owned and managed by the Woodland Trust, there is a scar of limestone on the right which becomes adorned with an interesting selection of flowers in the spring. Everyone loves the primroses which flower so early in the year, a sign of warmer days ahead. Then a few weeks later comes its cousin, the rarer though no less beautiful cowslip, with its drooping, multiple flower-heads. The woods of oak, ash and sycamore have well-spaced, tall trees, making an attractive setting for a fine display of bluebells in May. Continue to the upper end of the wood where there is a splendid view of the gravel banks in the river and some good birdwatching in the spring. It is easy to stand behind a tree to watch, among others, the redshank and the common sandpiper. The redshank is not so numerous as the sandpiper, but is a larger wader with a much more striking white bar on the wing and a handsome pair of red legs. The base of the bill is also red. It has a clear 'tu-tu-tu' call. Although these two waders often

Redshank.

'vanish' among the pebbles, they will soon reveal themselves after a short wait.

Make your way up to the road and cross into Grass Wood. This much larger, denser wood is owned and managed by the Yorkshire Wildlife Trust, who have been generous enough to allow us to walk along this lower part of the wood, although it is not an official right of way.

After a short climb turn left. The path runs parallel to the road. Along this stretch there are hosts of the attractively-named lily of the valley, for which the wood is famous. The diminutive, pure white bell-shaped flowers are of unusual delicacy and give off a delightfully sweet fragrance. The broad green leaves make a bright background for these exquisite blooms. Many people grow cultivated lily of the valley in their gardens, and the scent is emulated in perfumes and soaps.

Turn up to the right at the end of the wood where, to the left, there is a way out onto the road. It was here that Dr Petty, the GP of Grassington, was foully murdered by Tom Lee, blacksmith and poacher, in the year 1766. Tom Lee was not convicted until two years later, when his body was hung in gibbet irons at this very spot. The garters were adorned with silver buckles, but these were soon stolen. The bleached bones hung there for four years or more. A short way up the track there is lovely view up the dale through a gap in the trees. Beneath the beeches grow bluebells, dog's mercury and wild garlic.

Especially in the autumn, many kinds of fungi grow in the woods, often spectacular in colour and shape. They make a fascinating study as they can be totally unpredictable. Some may appear regularly but it is possible to find a rare one which may not reappear for a great many years.

Keep on up the hill until the small path bears round to the right, past moss-covered limestone pavements, straggly bushes of guelder rose and white-flowered bird cherry. The white blooms of guelder rose are like those of hydrangea, but with larger outer flowers, which are infertile and open first. In the autumn the shiny red berries are very conspicuous. Wood sage has wrinkled leaves and is the food plant of the speckled yellow moth. This is an unmistakable day-flying moth, a deep yellow, dappled with dark patches. In Yorkshire it was originally only found in Grass Wood, though it has more recently been found further afield. As you walk along the path you may come across a slow-worm basking in the dappled sunlight. The most likely time to see them do this is when they come out of hibernation in March. The slow-worm is a legless lizard, looks like a small snake and is quite harmless. They would be most useful in the garden, as they are slug-eaters.

Birds to listen or look out for include the nuthatch with its repetitive whistle, a call that frequently varies. It is more easily seen before the leaves are on the trees. The name comes from its habit of wedging nuts in the bark of a tree and splitting them with its 'hatchet' bill. Another all-year resident is the tree creeper, a little smaller than the nuthatch; it is brown above and silvery-white beneath. It can be recognised by its habit of crawling up the trunk of a tree in short spurts as it probes with its curved bill for insects. If you hear the hammering sound of a woodpecker, it is likely to be the great spotted woodpecker, as the green woodpecker habitually feeds on the ground looking for ants, though you may hear the laughing 'yaffle' of the latter.

Keep to the left of the 'settlement' for Park Stile and the way back through the fields via Cove Lane into Grassington. This prehistoric site is an Iron Age settlement similar to ones higher up on Lea Green. It has become covered with trees and thick vegetation and is not easy to see.

WALK 10: MOSSDALE SCAR FROM GRASSINGTON

Start: Grassington, the square. Grid Ref: 002 640
Distance: 7½ miles (12km)
OS Maps: Outdoor Leisure 10 or Landranger 98
Walking Time: 4 hours

This is a fine upland walk, mostly on limestone or good tracks, so is generally dry underfoot. Evidence of man's activities over the centuries is apparent all along. The walk joins the Bycliffe road, visits Mossdale Scar and its disappearing beck, and returns along the Dales Way. There are splendid panoramic views from these high-level footpaths. There are three car parks in Grassington which avoid the busy square.

Grassington is good place to look for dates and letters on lintels over doorways, and become a doorway spotter. Just below the square, the fine old building of Church House has the date and initials 'S.A.P. 1694'. The letters stand for the Christian names and surname of the couple who lived there and, according to Elizabeth Raistrick, this yeoman's house belonged to Stephen and Alice Peart. In Pletts Fold, off the bottom of Main Street, an inscription reads 'H.E.A. 1744', and at the end of Chapel Street one building is dated 1628. A shop on Main Street was the smithy of Tom Lee, Dr Petty's murderer, and Pletts Barn higher up the village – now the Mountaineer – was a preaching place of John Wesley.

From the square go up Main Street past Tom Lee's 'smiddy', left along Chapel Street then right up Bank Lane, signed 'Bare House and Bycliffe Road'. At the end of the lane, turn right and over a stile to enter a long narrow pasture, with a squeezer stile at the top. Already here on Kimper Hill you get an excellent view of the dale, with Grass Wood just below and Threshfield to the left. The quarries on the other side of the valley seem to stand out on this walk. You can see Cracoe and Skirethorns quarries, and later the third working quarry at Kilnsey comes into view. The one at Cracoe is the biggest eyesore but the

other two are mostly well-hidden. All three create polluting grey dust in dry weather.

Over the next stile is the last remaining wall of a former house, which looks as though it might fall down any day. Beds of nettles, often suggesting former human habitation, grow well here. They like the nitrate-rich soil where chamber pots have been emptied or kitchen waste thrown, but they also have strong, spreading yellow roots which invade untended gardens.

We are now in the centre of a large area of 'Celtic fields'. Once you are familiar with the tell-tale signs, you can pick out field boundaries, and if there is a dusting of snow or the sun is low in the sky, the ridges of the field system show up better. Most of the fields are Romano-British, dating from 100 to 300 AD, and cover an area of over 250 acres (100ha). They consist of a network of oblong fields, varying in size from 100 yards long and 20 yards wide to smaller shapes with narrow roadways and long boundary walls. Further south on Lea Green, on the return path, there is an entire village of rectangular huts within a defensive wall. The remains are not easy to pick out and are best studied from aerial photographs.

From the gable ruin, a footpath sign and stile can be seen ahead and beyond that a ladder stile. The route has now left the

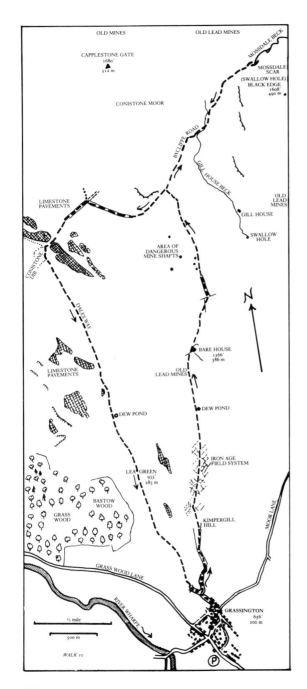

OLD MINES

OLD LEAD MINES

MOSSDALE BECK

CAPPLESTONE GATE
1680'
512 m

MOSSDALE
SCAR
(SWALLOW HOLE)
BLACK EDGE
1608'
490 m

CONISTONE MOOR

BYCLIFFE ROAD

GILL HOUSE BECK

OLD
LEAD
MINES

LIMESTONE
PAVEMENTS

GILL HOUSE

SWALLOW
HOLE

CONISTONE DIB

AREA OF
DANGEROUS
MINE SHAFTS

N

DALES WAY

BARE HOUSE
1266'
386 m

LIMESTONE
PAVEMENTS

OLD
LEAD MINES

DEW POND

DEW POND

IRON AGE
FIELD SYSTEM

LEA GREEN
935'
285 m

BASTOW
WOOD

GRASS
WOOD

KIMPERGILL
HILL

MOOR LANE

GRASS WOOD LANE

RIVER WHARFE

GRASSINGTON
656'
200 m

½ mile

500 m

WALK 10

P

74

Grassington.

ancient field system and entered the edge of a large and scattered leadmining area; just before the ladder stile are some old mine shafts that look like small craters. It is important from here to find the correct path, so take the old track to the left of that signposted, and pass a beautifully-walled dewpond which, in spite of a cemented lining, often contains no water. On the skyline can be seen two enormous perched boulders left stranded by the ice; there are other smaller ones to look out for. Exit this pasture at the top corner by a gated stile, and here a large pile of stones marks an area of mine shafts. There are tremendous views across the dale from here, especially just below, where the rock surface of the tree-dotted limestone pavements of Dib Scar stare up at you.

Barras or Bare House, from the Norse *bargh-hus* meaning hill farm, was a well-equipped sheep farm and has only been deserted in recent years. The name Bare House was mistakenly introduced by mapmakers on early Ordnance Survey maps. The original homestead was founded by Viking settlers, and the present building is a typical Dales long house, with the house on the left and the cows and barn on the right, all under the same roof. Don't follow the sign to Conistone, but continue behind the empty farmhouse and past the corner of a stone wall along a well-defined cart track, still in the same up-valley direction. (Another path branches off to the right here to High Barn.)

This is good bird country, and from March lapwings seem to be tumbling out of the sky in their acrobatic flight, skylarks are on the wing in full-throated song, while the call of the curlew is never far away. The display of the curlew is one of the great sights and sounds of the moors. The male rises steeply into the air, wings beating rapidly, hovers for a moment and then descends on stiff vibrating wings, letting out a thrilling series of calls, bubbling and piping and finishing with the melancholy 'coor-lew' which gives it its name. The curlew is much quieter when incubating its eggs, and the adult birds will change places on the nest in cautious silence. When the eggs have hatched, however, the parents become much more noisy and aggressive, and will chase after intruders.

Curlew.

The right of way leaves the cart track to a step stile in the wall on the right, across a field corner, to a gate which leads onto a short section of green lane running along the brow of the hill; then through another gate, past a tip heap. With care, take a look in the centre of this spoil heap to see a well-built, open and dangerous mine shaft, growing with ferns. There is another further on and a natural pothole as well, so go carefully!

Climb the ladder stile past another line of old shafts, and across open fell and a rabbit-proof fence. This replaces a broken wall in which there are splendid examples of fossil crinoids. The crinoid was an animal very common in the tropical seas of Carboniferous times. It lived on a long stalk and even had a sort of root to keep it upright, with many arms which it waved about, directing food particles down to its mouth. It is very rare for the crinoid 'head' to be preserved, and it is almost always the stem and arms that are found fossilised. They look like segmented worms and have the common name of sea-lily.

You now join the Bycliffe road that leads to Mossdale Scar. Turn right here for a moorland walk a long way from any civilisation, but easy going along this old packhorse route that goes over into Nidderdale. You may not see another soul. The path leads through green limestone pastures and on to millstone grit country, fords Gill House Beck and eventually arrives at a cliff of Yoredale limestone. It is only at the last moment that Mossdale Beck comes into view in its final stages. This sizable stream then vanishes completely at the foot of the overhanging cliff, among large blocks of limestone. It is an impressive sight and the best example of a disappearing stream in the Dales. The squarish blocks of stone have accumulated from rockfalls from the fifty foot (15m) high scar above. A close look at the limestone blocks reveals some large fossil shells embedded in them. These are the lampshell Gigantoproductus. The pure calcite shells look thick and glassy where they have been dissolved by rainwater.

Mossdale once attracted many potholers, and in his book *Yorkshire Dales: Limestone Country*, Tony Waltham describes the very sad caving tragedy that occurred here on the 24th June 1967, when six young and experienced cavers died in Mossdale Caverns. The small, 1,000 yard long Marathon Passage acts as an overflow for the main stream, and because it is so small can be rapidly filled to the roof with floodwater. The six cavers were on their way back along this tight crawl when, above ground, an intense rainstorm turned the beck into a raging torrent. The ensuing floodwaters rushed along the overflow to meet them. All six drowned and a plaque has been placed above the now-sealed entrance as a tribute to their memory.

Return along the Bycliffe road, which after one mile enters a walled section to a crossroads. Turn left down the hill and get an unexpected view of the tops of two limestone pavements which are tilted towards you, between which is the ravine of Conistone Dib. Just beyond the gate there is an old dewpond on the right, and further over a limekiln comes into view. It is a most scenic spot. Pass between the pavements and turn left through the gate and across the top of the Dib. The route back to Grassington is the Dales Way.

From a few paces along the path there is a good view on the right of Conistone Dib, while on the left are traces of Iron Age fields. Make for the step stile which is reddened by the colour of the soil from people's boots. Why red soil? Soils on limestone are often red because of the iron oxides in them. Heavy rainfall dissolves soluble salts in the soil and leaves clay impurities, rich in iron, giving the soil a reddish colour. You can see the redness, too, in the molehills. The flower that benefits from this condition is one of the most beautiful in the dale, the yellow mountain pansy. There are hundreds of them along here from the middle of May to the end of June. By July there are the delicate yellow flowers of the rockrose and tiny white starry heads of fairy flax and limestone bedstraw.

Continue along this pleasant route past an old limekiln built of huge blocks of stone and one or two limestone pavements to a ladder stile, which brings you onto Lea Green, a large pasture with many interesting features. First, about 100 yards (90m) on the left is a dewpond, which for generations must have provided valuable water for grazing animals. Opposite this is a burial mound or cairn. Nearby on a limestone pavement is a Romano-British 'village' of oblong hut shapes, bounded by an enclosing wall. It is likely that the dewpond was their water supply, as it is fed by a small spring. There are plenty of molehills on Lea Green, though the mole itself is rarely seen, spending most of its time underground. However, they do come to the surface, mainly at night, to collect dry grass and leaves for making a nest. Their main food is earthworms, of which they eat half their bodyweight each day. Further along there are two lines of pits, marking lead veins which cross the path. The mining was a simple, early type where small pits and trenches were dug into the vein from the surface. The workings can be seen to follow a straight line at an angle to the footpath. Keep to the double track to approach Grassington along a narrow, walled green lane.

WALK 11: CAPPLESTONE GATE FROM CONISTONE

Start: Conistone. Grid Ref: 981 674
Distance: 10½ miles (17km)
OS Maps: Outdoor Leisure 10 or Landranger 98
Walking Time: 5½ hours

Starting at Conistone village, three miles north of Grassington, the walk goes up the Dib and continues up the fellside to a magnificent viewpoint, with a climb of over 1,000 feet (300m). It passes the old leadmines of Capplestone Gate, and returns along the high-level path to Conistone. There are lovely views and some very fine limestone scenery. Parking is rather limited in the village and there is more space by the bridge.

Conistone is a very attractive and unspoilt collection of farms, cottages and barns built of limestone and grouped haphazardly round a small green. The name given by the Anglian settlers means a 'farmstead of cows', and it is mentioned in the *Domesday Book*. Many of the buildings are late seventeenth century, a few with dated lintels. Some of the barns have been converted into comfortable homes, and there are still occasional dovecotes to be seen in the gable ends. Arthur Raistrick in his *Old Yorkshire Dales* presented a detailed history of a farmhouse in Conistone. The house is just opposite the path to Grassington, and has an added porch with a lintel inscribed 'WR 1894' over the door. Built about the 1550s, it was extended and enlarged in 1687 and is described as a yeoman farmer's house. The village is even quieter now, having lost its post office, shop and cafe. Above the village is some of the finest limestone scenery in Wharfedale, beginning with Conistone Dib and opening out to limestone scars, pavements and fells.

The Dib is a classic example of the dry valley. Towards the end of the Ice Age, when the ground was still deep-frozen, no water could sink down, even into the limestone. The climate was getting warmer, and in the springs and summers there were torrents of rushing water from the melting snow and ice on the fells, which poured relentlessly down Conistone Dib (and other gills) and into the valley below, which may have had a lake in it for a time. On reaching the main valley, the dashing stream came to a sudden halt and dropped its load of gravel and sand in a sloping, fan-shaped delta. This gravel patch is the site of the village. It is above flood level and has good water supplies. Kettlewell, Starbotton and Buckden are also sited on similar gravel patches.

From the green, make for the white house between lines of stones. The last house is the Old School House, and the sign at the gate reads 'Conistone Dib'. The Dib soon narrows into the tight gorge of Gurling Trough which zigzags as it follows first one direction of natural joints in the rock, then the other. At the narrowest point it is just over two feet (65 cm) wide and you can see how the water once surged down the steep course, carving its channel as it went. All the water is now underground and no stream flows down the Dib today. The valley soon opens out, with coarse limestone screes on the slopes. It is here in spring you may see your first mountain pansy, showing its yellow face in the grass, along with milkwort, violet, germander speedwell and tormentil. The diminutive milkwort attracts attention by its rich deep

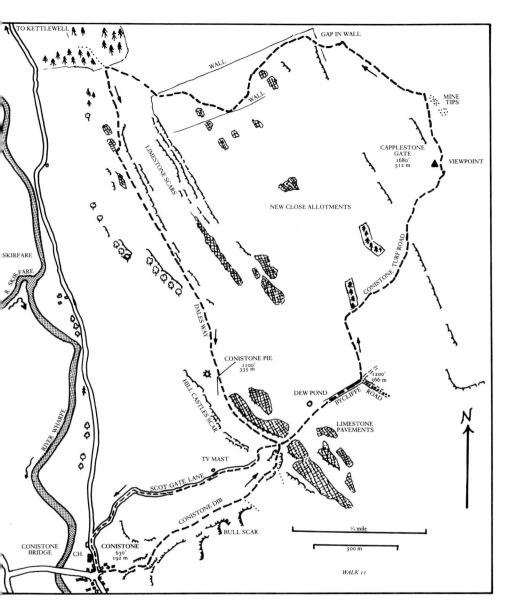

blue or purple colour and its unusually-shaped flowers, which are worth a closer look using a lens. a tiny tube of petals is almost concealed by two large blue sepals.

In summer the large purple heads of greater knapweed are here, as well as the bluish-lilac flowers of small scabious.

79

Limestone pavement above Conistone Dib.

The Dib then narrows again, with a short scramble up the last few feet to the top. Climb over the stile and turn left over the gritstone slabs and go through the gate. Turn right along the track signed 'Mossdale'. But first step up the low scar near the path and take a look at a piece of amazing limestone pavement. The odd ash or hawthorn tree, which incredibly grow out of cracks in the rock, seem to accentuate the desolate, flat, fretted surface. It may appear deserted, but look between the blocks for a wealth of limestone plants growing in the shelter of the grikes. Here is a natural rock garden where you can make some interesting discoveries. Hart's tongue fern is the first you will recognise, rooted deep in the grike. Another fern you may find, if you look carefully, is the small maidenhair spleenwort, which differs from the green spleenwort in having a black stem rather than a green one. The small geranium herb robert is common, and has red leaves where there is most light near the surface of the pavement, and green in the deeper shade. Tufts of wall rue grow from cracks near the top of the grikes, and three-fingered saxifrage with its tiny white flowers can be found near the surface of the pavement. Bigger ferns include male fern, broad buckler fern and the delicate lady fern.

Continue in the direction of higher ground along the cart track past a dewpond on the left, after which there is a short walled section to a crossroads of green lanes. Signed 'Capplestone Gate', the double track to the left passes near to two small conifer plantations and then crosses a

Herb robert.

line of old mine shafts. In the path the fossil lamp shell *Gigantoproductus* can be seen again, the biggest and thickest fossil shell you are likely to come across. There is a sudden change in geology and vegetation as a capping of millstone grit is reached. Here the white pillar of the trig point at Capplestone Gate, 1,680 feet (512m) above sea level, affords an extensive panorama up dale and down, with Great Whernside and Buckden Pike on the right and Wharfedale and Littondale below. Go through the gate and take the Kettlewell

path along a shallow edge of grit. Ahead are leadmine spoil heaps, where minerals of calcite, fluorite and barite may be found. The miners discarded these three whitish minerals and referred to them as 'gangue' – waste material. Barite is the only really heavy white mineral. It can be distinguished by its platy structure, rather like a disorderly pack of cards. When ground up, it is the stuff a barium meal is made from, since being so dense it shows up on an X-ray plate. Fluorite is less heavy and often looks watery rather than white. You can also find galena here, the ore of lead, and even bits of coal from a coal pit. In digging out the levels and shafts the miners brought up quantities of limestone and in some pieces are fragments of the giant lamp shell again.

Take the left path downhill from the signpost and over a ladder stile. After a second ladder stile, turn left to head towards the valley. The path enters a very large pasture through a broken-down section of wall, then swings left. It crosses an old worked vein, passes near to some limestone pavements then, after reaching the left hand wall, turns right to a gate at the bottom right hand corner. There are rabbits everywhere, including one or two completely black ones. Rabbits were introduced into Britain from the Continent in the twelfth century for their valuable meat and skins, but only became common in the last 200 years. One female rabbit can produce twenty offspring in a year and numbers sometimes reach plague proportions.

From the gate, aim for the lower end of the conifer plantation but, instead of going into the wood, turn left along the Dales Way back to the top of Conistone Dib. The path follows a shelf of land high above the valley and below a limestone scar, with great views below of the junction of Littondale and Wharfedale and the flat floor of the former lake bed. The yellow mountain pansy is in its element here, and several ancient walls cross the path at right angles. Coniston Pie soon comes into view. This wonderful, natural pie-shaped rock retains the same outline from whichever side you view it. The cairn on the top, representing the pie funnel, completes its unique shape. Climb onto the rock for a fine view which looks along the trough shapes of each of the two dales. Ahead is Kilnsey Crag and Kilnsey village, with Mastiles Lane disappearing up the fellside. To the right is the cliff of Blue Scar in Littondale.

The walk continues by climbing the ladder stile behind Coniston Pie, and is joined by another scar on the left. Here and there are ancient sloping tracks cut into the scar to gain the next level. On reaching the signpost, turn right down Scot Gate Lane past the TV mast and steeply down Wassa Bank towards Conistone. As you pass the church, step into the churchyard to view a memorial stone to the six young men who died in Mossdale Caverns. The peaceful interior of the church is worth a visit to see two perfect Norman arches opposite the door. The bases of these arches are said to be even more ancient. On the wall is a poem in memory of the six cavers, and there are many plaques to the Tennant family of Chapel House.

WALK 12: KILNSEY, MASTILES LANE AND THE CRAVEN FAULT

Start: Conistone Bridge. Grid Ref: 979 675
Distance: 10½ miles (17km)
OS Maps: Outdoor Leisure 10 or Landranger 98
Walking Time: 5½ hours

Conistone Bridge on the River Wharfe is three miles (5km) north of Grassington, and makes a convenient starting point for this walk which explores Kilnsey Crag, Mastiles Lane and the line of the Craven Fault between Bordley and Skirethorns. Though fairly long, it is easy going and can be shortened if necessary (see map). There is limited parking along the roadside by Conistone Bridge or in the village.

Kilnsey Crag is the most spectacular limestone feature in Wharfedale. Its great bulk dominates everything around, its sphinx-like form guarding the upper dale. The Crag is 140 feet (40m) high and the overhang projects a record thirty feet (10m). It is a favourite with experienced rock climbers, and the overhang was first scaled using artificial aid in 1957. The route became known as Mandela as it was thought it would never go 'free', but it was free-climbed on the 16th September 1989 by the incredible Mark Leach from Lancashire.

The Crag was created by the action of the Wharfedale glacier, which cut off projecting spurs of land in its straightening and deepening course down the valley, leaving a vertical face of rock. Another such truncated spur occurs higher up the valley at Blue Scar in Littondale. At a later stage a smaller glacier may have undercut the Crag to produce the overhang. The perfectly flat 'flood plain' of the valley floor here at Kilnsey contrasts sharply with the majestic Crag.

The best approach is on foot along the path from Conistone Bridge, allowing a fine head-on view of this towering mass of rock. Start by going through the stile on the left side of the bridge when facing up-stream. The sign very appropriately is for Scar Laithe, the name of the barn at the foot of the Crag which you can see across the fields. The local word 'laithe' means barn, and Kilnsey Scar is the former name of the Crag. The path is indistinct but passes across the corner of three walled fields on the left and heads straight for the barn, where it comes out onto the road. It is in these fields that the Kilnsey Show, now held in late August each year, provides many traditional events such as sheepdog trials, horse trotting, drystone walling and a race to the top of the Crag, besides the showing of sheep and cattle. It has become one of the biggest and most popular shows in Wharfedale.

For a closer look, cross the road and walk up alongside the crystal-clear stream that flows the length of the Crag. You will marvel at the amazing feats of the intrepid rock climbers in their colourful gear, and wonder at their strength and ingenuity to cling to this awesome rockface. Go to the source of the unbelievably clear rushing waters at the far end of the Crag, where there are three or four powerful springs. Here is a profusion of flowers, with banks of delicate primroses, violets, early purple orchids and mossy saxifrage. The ground here is boggy, with bunches of brilliant

Conistone, Kilnsey Crag and Old Cote Moor.

yellow kingcups, dainty birdseye primroses, lady's smock and watercress. In the summer the deep yellow monkey flower provides a new splash of colour, an incomer which looks part of the scene. On the crag itself nest house martins and jackdaws.

Retrace your steps and proceed to the Tennant Arms, which is just as much a part of Kilnsey as the Crag or the show, and takes its name from a long line of the Tennant family who lived in this area. Go up the narrow lane to the left of the Tennant Arms, where you see Kilnsey Old Hall. Only the shell of this splendid old building remains, with its mullioned windows, limestone walls and lofty appearance. It was built in 1648 and, although now used as a barn, it still retains some of the dignity

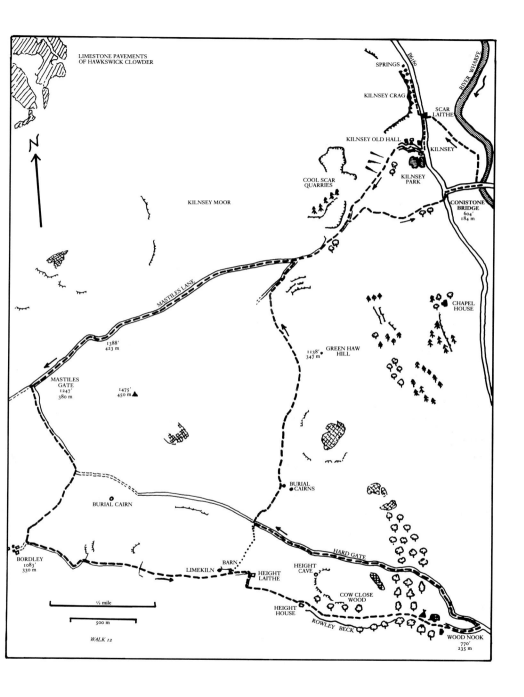

LIMESTONE PAVEMENTS
OF HAWKSWICK CLOWDER

N

SPRINGS

KILNSEY CRAG

SCAR
LAITHE

BECK

RIVER WHARFE

KILNSEY OLD HALL

KILNSEY

COOL SCAR
QUARRIES

KILNSEY
PARK

KILNSEY MOOR

CONISTONE
BRIDGE
604'
184 m

CHAPEL
HOUSE

MASTILES LANE

1388'
423 m

1138'
347 m

GREEN HAW
HILL

MASTILES
GATE
1247'
380 m

1475'
450 m ▲

BURIAL
CAIRNS

BURIAL CAIRN

BORDLEY
1083'
330 m

HARD GATE

LIMEKILN

BARN

HEIGHT
LAITHE

HEIGHT
CAVE

COW CLOSE
WOOD

½ mile

HEIGHT
HOUSE

ROWLEY BECK

500 m

WOOD NOOK
770'
235 m

WALK 12

85

it had when Lady Anne Clifford stayed there in 1663 on her journey north. The Old Hall was built on the site of the principal grange of Fountains Abbey. A portion of the original gate house of the grange still remains, with filled-in, rounded windows. The grange was the management centre of the large sheep ranches in Wharfedale.

Proceed up the road and Kilnsey Park fish ponds come into view down on the left, where fishermen are likely to make a catch and where visitors can see and feed the trout at various stages of growth. On the right is the entrance to Kilnsey's working quarry and the bare limestone crags of Cool Scar. Further on, beyond a wooden gate, the road is bound on both sides by some beautiful drystone walling which snakes in a double line up the fellside of Kilnsey Moor into the distance. Below your feet the road is very well paved with small cobbles of limestone. This is Mastiles Lane, the most famous of the ancient monastic routes which linked Fountains Abbey with its granges at Malham and its estates in Cumbria. It is difficult to imagine that, in the twelfth and thirteenth century, merchant princes from Florence and Venice with their attendants and all their finery travelled along this route when they came to buy the quality wool of the Fountains estates.

Over the brow of the hill, which lies 1,390 feet (423m) above sea level, descend to Mastiles Gate. Go through the gate and turn left off the green road and along a shallow dry valley with a wall on the left. At the end of the wall, bear right and take the farm road to Bordley. The OS map shows seven footpaths meeting at Bordley, an indication of its importance in former times. In the seventeenth century there were over a hundred people living in this community. It was part of the Fountains Abbey estate, had close ties with Wharfe-dale and was part of Burnsall parish.

Just before Bordley Farm, turn left along another wall signed 'Threshfield'. From here there is an inviting view south of the Winterburn Valley and its reservoir, while to the east is a view along the Craven Fault. On one side of the fault are limestone crags and the familiar short green turf, while on the right is rough grassland, a shade darker than that on the limestone, with occasional outcrops of black shale. From here for the next mile or so the path follows more or less the line of the Craven Fault. Look for evidence of limestone and basic soils on the left and shales or millstone grit and acid soils on the right. Note the material of which the walls are built (grit or limestone), and the contrast in vegetation between one side of the fault and the other. The fault follows a dip between higher ground; this makes sense since it is a line of weakness, therefore more easily eroded.

At the end of the first pasture from Bordley, bear left to find a stile over the wall – a limestone wall with gritstone slabs in the stile – and continue up the steep hill past two water troughs carved out of grit. Here you can see the abrupt change in vegetation due to the fault. Make for a ladder stile near a ruined limekiln. Looking ahead, the reef knolls and Thorpe Fell come into view, both of which are to the right or south side of the fault. To the left of these, in a limestone scar, you can see the large double entrance of Heights Cave.

Make for the barn in the field corner, but before you get there, notice on the left what must be the best-preserved limekiln in Wharfedale. It has a narrow arch, but still has the iron grid in place from which the burnt lime was raked. Growing in the shelter of the kiln is the small fern, green spleenwort. Restricted to limestone, it can be distinguished from common or maiden-hair spleenwort by its green rather than black stem. The barn is also of interest, with its arched doorways and windows, and exterior stone steps to the hay loft above.

From here it is possible to shorten the walk by turning left, cutting out the walk through Wood Nook. Otherwise, cross the lane and continue straight on to Height Laithe where you must turn right, then left, to reach the abandoned farmhouse of Height House. The path passes to the left of the building as it makes its way between Cow Close Wood on the left and Rowley Beck, which runs along the Craven Fault. Patches of Bowland shale can be seen on the far side of the beck, with limestone outcrops on the near side. This is an ancient open woodland of ash, hazel, silver birch and hawthorn, with some interesting wild flowers, especially at the campsite. Here there is a wonderful array among the trees, including wood anemone, wood sorrel, bluebell, early purple orchid and dog violet; a little later in the summer there are rockrose, wood cranesbill, goldilocks and hairy St John's wort. Comfrey grows at the car park, a plant that has been used for centuries to help set broken bones – as its old name of knitbone implies. The long tubular flowers which hang down in bunches vary in colour from purple or blue to pink or white, and only insects with long tongues can reach the nectar.

Proceed through the caravans to Wood Lane. Turn left for a pleasant walk up the hill amongst the blackthorn which in April, before the leaves come out, is a show of lovely white blossom, and by the end of October hangs with a mass of black sloes with their wonderful waxy bloom. The road follows a dry valley, and at the top of the hill there is a possibility of visiting Height Cave on the left, a short way along the farm track to Height House. The most impressive part of the cave is the double-arched entrance with a natural limestone pillar and sculptured roof, beyond which there is little depth to the cave. There is a local tradition that a company of Bonny Prince Charlie's men sheltered in the cave on their long and miserable retreat north during the Jacobite Rebellion. It was a wintery December in 1745 and it is said that a few men were welcomed by Dales folk and never experienced their defeat at Culloden.

Continue along the road for another third of a mile (½ km), to where there is the crossing of an ancient routeway with a gate on each side of the road. The gateposts here are interesting. The one on the left, made of gritstone, has a square hole in it, and the two gateposts on the right have a remarkable surface of large rounded quartz pebbles, typical of the Grassington grit. Go through this gate, where the path is waymarked by posts with blue painted tops, denoting a bridleway, to another gate with a huge limestone gatepost. (One wonders how much gatepost is hidden below ground.) Even the gateway is paved to prevent too many animal feet from creating a quagmire. There are fine views along here of Buckden Pike and Great Whernside. Kilnsey quarry is straight ahead, where it has made a large hole in the Great Scar limestone. The track leads down to two gateways and onto Mastiles Lane at the point where it is no longer walled.

About 300 yards (275 m) along and opposite Cool Scar, there is a gateway on the right. Go through and skirt the gill to continue in roughly the same direction; curving to the right, join a farm track which leads to the main road, not far from Conistone Bridge, the starting point.

WALK 13: DOWBER GILL FROM KETTLEWELL

Start: Kettlewell. Grid Ref: 969 723
Distance: 4 miles (6km)
OS Maps: Outdoor Leisure 30 or Landranger 98
Walking Time: 2 hours or more

Here is a lovely walk, more of a stroll in a fascinating side valley. It takes in the secluded, flowery and geologically interesting ravine of Dowber Gill as far as Providence Pot, then returns from Hag Dike. There is a car park in the village.

Kettlewell is a fine stone-built village. Being on the edge of the early hunting forests in medieval times it grew as a forest market town, when it traded with the large monastic estates. In time the forests were cut down and Kettlewell became less imortant, relying on sheep farming, though it prospered for a short time from leadmining and the packhorse trade.

Today it is a popular centre for visitors, with its three pubs, the beck which runs between the houses, and the scenery of limestone scars and Great Whernside which look down on the attractive huddle of buildings. In 1869, B J Harker found Kettlewell '. . . anything but attractive, owing to there being so many cesspools, manure heaps and cow houses'. Things have improved a lot since then.

Go up the main street in front of the Bluebell Hotel and, at the post office, turn right over the bridge. The massive dressed topstones on this bridge are similar to those on Threshfield Bridge. Then turn left along a lane by the beck. The first half of the walk follows Dowber Gill Beck almost to its source. At the end of the lane, lined with sweet cicely, a sign points up a delightful narrow valley to Providence Pot.

This is Dowber Gill, a water-worn V-shaped valley with interlocking spurs (where the stream winds in and out between spurs of land) in contrast to the main U-shaped valley of the Wharfe which is

glaciated and has truncated spurs (cut off by glaciers).

The gill is particularly interesting for its geology. Not far along is a rare outcrop of sandstone, part of the Yoredale sequence of rocks, which in Wharfedale are chiefly limestones and shales (another outcrop of Yoredale sandstone appears on top of Parson's Pulpit). The steep grassy slopes of the ravine are covered in miniature terraces. These are formed by a combination of gravity and the action of sheep walking along them, and are locally known as sheep tracks. Beyond a pretty stepped waterfall, fossil crinoids and brachiopods are to be seen in the limestone and, on the right, steep scars and screes come into view. Lead-bearing mineral veins cross the valley and have been widely exploited.

This is also a spectacular place for wild flowers. On a summer's day the walk up to Providence Pot is like a botanical outing, and it is worth lingering over the flowers. In April there are primroses and cowslips, and the rich colour of early purple orchids. The bright blue germander speedwell and yellow tormentil add further colour. By the end of May there are three shades of common milkwort sharing the grassy slopes with bird's foot trefoil, salad burnet and dovesfoot cranesbill. The brilliantly coloured yellow rockrose is beginning to flower, and by June the deep pink cushions of wild thyme are everywhere. The yellow

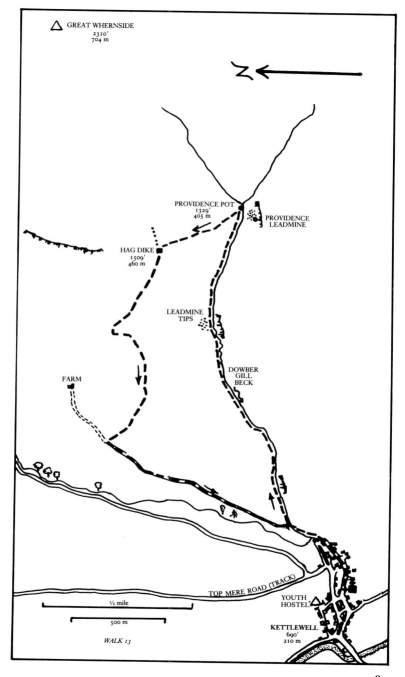

GREAT WHERNSIDE
2310'
704 m

PROVIDENCE POT
1329'
405 m

PROVIDENCE
LEADMINE

HAG DIKE
1509'
460 m

LEADMINE
TIPS

DOWBER
GILL
BECK

FARM

TOP MERE ROAD (TRACK)

YOUTH
HOSTEL

KETTLEWELL
690'
210 m

½ mile

500 m

WALK 13

Dowber Gill.

heads of hawkweeds and delicate white grass of Parnassus are also in bloom.

Often old tip heaps from leadmines never get covered over with vegetation because of the presence of the poisonous lead in the soil, and they can still be bare after a hundred years or more. However, the lead-tolerant, starry, white flowers of spring sandwort bring a sparkle to the spoil heaps. This plant is so closely associated with lead that it has been used as an indicator to find the ore and its other common name is leadwort. Some of the flowers may be pink, while others are pure white.

The old leadmine tip heaps contain various minerals which are exciting to find. There are clear forms of calcite, though crystals can be rather weathered. Calcite is the pure crystalline form of calcium carbonate of which limestone is made.

Crystals take on a six-sided shape, with either a blunt end known as 'nail head' or the sharper pointed 'dog tooth'. Lumps of calcite break up into rhomb shapes (like a slanting cube). Fluorite occurs as clear cubic crystals, one interlocking with another. Fluorite is heavier than calcite but not as heavy as barite. The miners referred to these three white sparry minerals as calc spar, fluor spar and heavy spar. They were waste to the miners, known as 'gangue' and thrown on the tip heaps. You may also find streaks of the green copper mineral malachite.

At Providence Mine there are good specimens of barite, with some galena and malachite. When Harker wrote about Kettlewell he said that the majority of its inhabitants were leadminers, 'among whom it is delightful to see an amount of intelligence and good sense.' In fact the mines

Spring sandwort.

of Dowber Gill were doing very well in the 1860s, when production reached a peak of 325 tons of lead ore in 1867.

A smelt mill was in operation at the foot of the gill, which was enlarged in 1868 and which used peat at seven shillings a ton to fire it. The mill came to a sad end in 1942 when it was blown up by the Army in a test explosion.

Providence Pot is a concrete manhole, with its own telephone wire right in the middle of the stream bed! This is a back door entrance to Dow Cave via the notorious Dowbergill Passage, an amazing and difficult mile long (1,600m) passage through the limestone, a caving classic by any standards and not for the inexperienced. Imagine a maze turned vertically. The Upper Wharfedale Fell Rescue Association have been called out more times to cavers who have lost their way in this passage than for any other pothole.

From Providence Pot turn sharp left up the steep, well-used path to Hag Dike, a former farmhouse and now scout centre for outdoor activities. (This section of the route is not an official right of way but is used by walkers.) In summer the harebell and foxglove are an indication of the more acid soils in this area. Keep a lookout overhead for the peregrine falcon which may be about. In the 1960s this was a very rare bird, having suffered from poison in the food chain when the spraying of DDT pesticides was widespread. This magnificent bird of prey has since made a remarkable recovery, and now breeds regularly in the Pennines. It may be seen soaring high over its hunting territory, or flap-glide-flap-glide as it progresses across the open sky.

From Hag Dike, 1,525 feet (465m) above sea level, descend via the vehicle track which winds down the hillside to join the walled lane above Cam Gill and return to Kettlewell, enjoying the changing views on the way.

WALK 14: KETTLEWELL TO ARNCLIFFE AND HAWKSWICK

Start: Kettlewell. Grid Ref: 969 723
Distance: 7½ miles (12km)
OS Maps: Outdoor Leisure 10 and 30 or Landranger 98
Walking Time: 4 hours

When it comes to the variety of birds, some beautiful wild flowers in an enchanting setting, and wonderful and changing views of two dales, this walk must rank as one of the best in this book. It involves a climb of nearly 1,000 feet (300m) over to Arncliffe and a short climb of 330 feet (100m) from Hawkswick. There is a car park in Kettlewell.

Lying in the deepest part of the dale, Kettlewell – meaning Ketil's spring – is in a superb setting, and makes a fine centre for the walker with inviting paths in all directions. It is a large village with a long history of sheep farming, leadmining and textiles. In the days when leadmining was at its peak, there was a cotton mill, five inns, three schools, three blacksmiths and a surgeon. Today Kettlewell is popular with visitors, and still has three hotels and other kinds of accommodation.

From the village, cross Kettlewell Bridge from where, in spring, you can see a fine display of cowslips on the far side of the river. Take the second gate on the right signed 'Arncliffe'. Leave the double track almost immediately to climb steeply up and get an amazing view back over the roof tops of Kettlewell. The path is waymarked and easy to follow up through a limestone scar, across a farm track and straight on up the hill, crossing the wall on the way. This is lapwing country, and in spring you could easily come across a nest or chicks. Up here the mountain pansy grows amongst the coarse grass and brightens up the hillside with its cheerful yellow colour.

Once over the ladder stile on the brow of the ridge, there is a fine view into Littondale and across to Parson's Pulpit, Blue Scar and the limestone pavements of Hawkswick Clouder. Littondale is a beau-

tiful valley, the typical Yorkshire dale. It has the almost straight glaciated trough shape, its own narrow side valleys, gills and quiet unspoilt villages, yet has a variety of scenery with woods and scars, and a peacefulness that make it just about perfect.

As you come down to an edge of limestone, where there is line of swallow holes, you get the full view into the dale with Arncliffe to the right. This limestone scar is frequented by ring ouzels, normally rather shy birds but you may hear the 'tac-tac-tac' of their alarm call or a piping 'peeu' as one perches on a distant rock. Ring ouzels are members of the thrush and blackbird family, but winter in southern Europe and north Africa. A little lower down, fossil corals outcrop on the path. They are mainly lithostrotion, the macaroni-shaped coral. In cross-section you can see the divisions radiating from the centre like the spokes of a wheel.

Descend over limestone scars and pastures in the direction of Arncliffe to the ancient woodland of Byre Bank Wood, an ash wood on limestone and a great place for spring flowers and birds. You can sit at the top and see the birds in the tree tops below you. Great spotted woodpeckers live here, and you may hear them drumming, when they are either feeding on insects in the bark of trees, or they may be signalling to one another as they tap out a loud rhythm

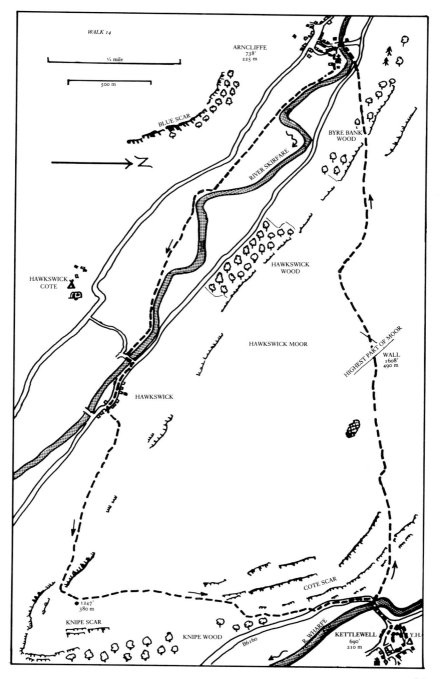

WALK 14

½ mile

500 m

Z

BLUE SCAR

ARNCLIFFE
738'
225 m

BYRE BANK
WOOD

RIVER SKIRFARE

HAWKSWICK
COTE

HAWKSWICK
WOOD

HAWKSWICK MOOR

HIGHEST PART OF MOOR

WALL
1608'
490 m

HAWKSWICK

COTE SCAR

1247'
380 m

KNIPE SCAR

KNIPE WOOD

B6160

R. WHARFE

KETTLEWELL
690'
210 m

Y.H.

Ring ouzel.

on a resonant dead branch. The drumming takes the place of song and identifies one individual to another, a sort of Morse Code. The ubiquitous willow warbler, too, inhabits the wood, as does the common redstart with its unmistakable fiery chestnut tail and robin-like flight, always on the move as it jumps from branch to branch.

Ash trees come late into leaf and even then allow plenty of light to reach the woodland floor, so a wealth of wild flowers grows here. The hillside is so steep that in the spring it has the look of a well-stocked rock garden. The earliest to show is dog's mercury. Dog violets also grow here – both names imply that they are only fit for dogs, dog's mercury being poisonous and dog violet having no scent. The popular primrose starts to flower in March, heralding the arrival of spring. It is one of five primulas that grow wild in Britain. Another is the cowslip which, like the primrose, has two sorts of flower, and pollen must be transferred from one to the other for fertile seeds to be produced. A third is the delicate pink birdseye primrose, which you may see on this walk if you look carefully in wet places.

Red campion likes the richer soils down near the bottom of the wood, and has separate plants for male and female flowers. The white-flowered bulbous wild garlic has leaves shaped like lily of the valley but with an oniony smell. A whole carpet of flowering garlic may brighten any wood, but gives off a powerful smell, different from the garlic used in cooking. Wood sage flowers in the summer with spikes of yellowish-green flowers on a square stem and wrinkled leaves that smell of hops. Early purple orchid has a rather loose spike of purple flowers and the leaves are often spotted, a flower closely associated with sex and love potions. However, it usually has an unpleasant cat smell.

Descend and cross the road, through the fields, past the church to the lovely village of Arncliffe. The attractive church with its solid fifteenth century tower stands in a perfect position by the Skirfare. Inside is a list of the thirty-four Littondale men who fought, along with their leader the Shepherd Lord, at Flodden Field in 1513. There is also a pike which may have been used at Flodden and a glass case containing a silver chalice made in 1619. The largest of the three bells is thought to date from 1350 and another is dated 1616. The church is the only one licensed for weddings in the dale.

Arncliffe is a very attractive old village, with its stone houses overlooking the large green. It certainly attracted the television cameras when the story of Emmerdale Farm was first filmed here. And it is no coincidence that the former name of the dale was Amerdale, which Wordsworth made use of in his epic poem of the White Doe. For Charles Kingsley – who stayed at

Bridge End, a house near the bridge – Littondale became Vendale when he was inspired to use the local river and dale scenery in the *The Water Babies*, in which little Tom met the water babies under the bridge next to the church.

From the church, take the path that leads through the fields to the right bank of the river. Just where the path leads away from the river over a stile, pause to look along this delightful stretch of the Skirfare for signs of dipper, wagtails and common sandpiper. There are views along here of another ancient ash wood, that of Hawkswick Wood on the left, and to the right are the cliffs of Blue Scar, frequented by climbers. Not far from Hawkswick, where the path rejoins the riverside again, in the summer you may see oystercatchers, redshank, sandpiper, pied, grey and yellow

wagtail, and dipper. It is quite easy along here to use the wall as a hide to watch unobserved. It is great to see the yellow wagtail, whose startling yellow makes the grey wagtail look dull! The tail is slightly shorter and the back a more greenish-brown, and it has a habit of perching on wire fences or posts, so you have a chance of a close look.

A footbridge over the Skirfare leads into Hawkswick, a pretty group of cottages, farms, old barns and converted barns strung out in a line more like a Wensleydale village than a Wharfedale one. The reason for this linear plan is the single road. There is no road junction around which houses would naturally cluster.

The path to Kettlewell is signposted and leads up the hillside, then diagonally upward to the ridge. Looking across

The view up Wharfedale from Kettlewell.

Littondale from here you can see a line of cairns which stand out on the skyline, and further on there is a clear view down into Wharfedale. You can make out the steep wooded sides of the Wharfe Valley, where it is particularly narrow, with Grass Wood to the left and Kilnsey Crag and Chapel House on the right. Once over the top the path changes course, and there are views up Wharfedale and into the valley of Cam Gill and Park Rash above Kettlewell. The refreshing changes of view in this walk are one of its main attractions.

On the way down, common dog violets dot the rough grassland, and the path descends the scars of the Yoredale limestones to woodland and an old track. The higher cliffs are the home of jackdaws, and screes have developed below them. The final 250 yards (230m) back to Kettlewell Bridge is along the road, but it is hoped there will be a safer alternative one day.

WALK 15: KETTLEWELL AND STARBOTTON

Start: Kettlewell. Grid Ref: 969 723
Distance: 5 miles (8km)
OS Maps: Outdoor Leisure 30 or Landranger 98
Walking Time: 2½ hours

This lovely walk in the upper part of Wharfedale boasts ever-changing views up and down the dale, and of the diminutive river as it makes its leisurely way along this glacial valley. The ancient wooded scars abound in a great variety of trees and flowers, and an old tip heap reveals its secrets. There is a fairly steep climb of 820 feet (250m) up to Moor End. Parking is available in Kettlewell.

The picturesque village of Kettlewell is a popular starting point for walkers, its buildings grouped round the beck in a setting that is the finest in Wharfedale. The history of the village goes back 700 years, when medieval Kettlewell had a weekly market with a charter granted in 1320 and became the main centre for upper Wharfedale. In those days it lay on the southern edge of the great hunting forests of Littondale and Langstrothdale, with the big monastery sheep estates to the south. After the dissolution, many of the farmers were able to own their own land as yeomen, which led to the building of stone farmhouses. There are a few of the old stone houses left – one has the date 1660 over the door – but most of them were rebuilt in the early nineteenth century when Kettlewell prospered from the leadmining industry and packhorse traffic, though the mines were closed by 1880.

The road from Kettlewell over Park Rash and into Coverdale is part of an ancient route from London to Richmond and is shown on Ogilby's maps of 1675. Branching from this, just above Kettlewell, is an old packhorse route along the green lane of Top Mere Road and Cam Head, which is so distinctive when viewed from the dale. This road goes to Top Mere peat grounds, with a continuation into Walden, West Burton and Wensleydale.

Go round the Bluebell Hotel up the street and continue past Cam Lodge on a grassy path between walls. A stile and a left turn along the wall brings you onto the up-valley footpath, with a front circle view of the finest stretch of this beautiful dale. Scattered ash, hazel, crab apple and hawthorn decorate the slopes, especially in late spring when the stunted thorn trees become a mass of creamy may blossom. Tree seedlings tend to get eaten by sheep, but the hawthorn has a second method of reproduction by sending out suckers which are strong and thorny, and so survive. Many of the hawthorn trees are very old, and they often grow in lines or groups which reflect this way of multiplying.

Nearer Starbotton the way goes left through a green gate and diagonally down to the village. Starbotton sees all the traffic which comes up or down the dale passing along the one road. Yet the village has the appearence of a rather quiet community, with stone-built farms, houses and cottages of an age gone by, most of the buildings being more than 150 years old. But there is activity and an atmosphere of restoration, conversion and construction bringing it into the late twentieth century.

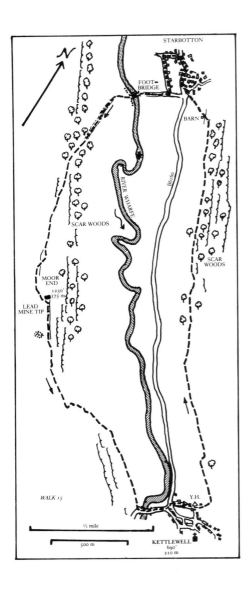

typical location for a village, like those of Kettlewell, Buckden, Litton and many more. However, its very situation was to be its downfall 300 years ago when, on the 8th June 1686, a torrential downpour in the Cam Gill area flooded the village, bringing down tons of gravel and mud, destroying some cottages, filling others with debris and covering acres of good farmland. Damage was estimated at £3,000 and money was raised on a national level to help the distressed inhabitants. Some of the houses were fairly new then, with dates of 1663 and 1665. In July 1667, Lady Anne Clifford stayed the night here on her journey north to Pendragon Castle in Mallerstangdale.

Go through the village and turn left alongside the beck, then over the bridge and back along a lane of barns. Turn right at the end to the footbridge over the Wharfe, where a depth of water indicator shows we are 213 metres (700 feet) above sea level. Go straight on here, through the wooden gate signed 'Arncliffe' along an old track up through the woods. This monastic route follows the Monks Road from Malham to Arncliffe over Old Cote Moor, down by this path to Starbotton, then over to Coverdale. Most of the land belonged to Fountains Abbey, with a grange on Malham Moor. This little stretch, with its narrow winding way between two low ruined walls, certainly has the look and feel of a time-worn and ancient monkish path. The woods are fairly thick here, containing mainly hazel with a few ash, blackthorn, and bird cherry. The last two trees both have white blossom – blackthorn in March and bird cherry in May – and splashes of white dot the hillside at the appropriate season. There is a wonderful view from higher up of the meandering Wharfe in the valley below, and looking down the dale the stepped outline of the successive limestone scars of the Yoredales.

The village stands on a gravel patch where Cam Gill Beck enters the dale. Such a position is above the flood level of the River Wharfe, and water supplies are easily obtained from wells or from the beck. It is a

Kettlewell.

Follow the footpath signs through Moor End. This building, dating from about 1700, was built for the manager of the nearby leadmines. It was a working farm for several generations, well-known the length of the dale and now, in the leisure era, it is used by the Bradford and District Outward Bound Association and the Duke of Edinburgh Award Club.

Go through the yard and keep the wall on the left. At the other end of this field is the large tip heap of Moor End Mine. Rabbits have made their home in the soft sandy spoil, and plant life has been slow to get established on the lead-poisoned soil. The mine worked three lead veins in the limestone and sent ore to a smelt mill in Starbotton. The shaft reached a depth of 210 feet (65m), and one of the veins was worked over a horizontal distance of 700 yards (650m).

Have a look here for a few interesting minerals. You should find galena – lead sulphide, the ore of lead. It looks dull grey when weathered and is much heavier than the other minerals. When broken it shines a silvery grey and, on refining, usually provides a small percentage of silver. Clear cubic crystals of fluorite – calcium fluoride – are easy to identify, the watery cubes being interbedded with each other; even easier is the Blue John, the purple variety, with a wonderful deep purple colour. Fluorite is used as a flux in the steel industry and in ceramic glazes. Barite – the chemical composition being barium sulphate – is white and heavy, and some specimens at this mine are a pale pink. The

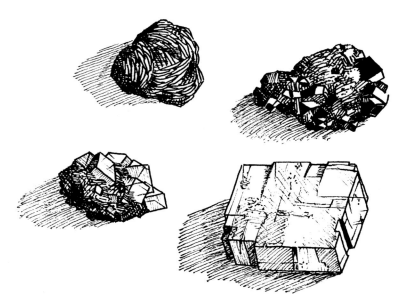

Minerals (clockwise from top left): barite, galena, calcite and fluorite.

platy crystals may be found together with cubes of purple fluorite and make an attractive specimen. Barite is used as a filler in paints and paper. When finely ground it is used in drilling mud for the drilling of oil wells. Calcite – calcium carbonate – is also present in rather weathered crystals. Re-deposited lime in the form of flowstone, the material of stalactites and stalagmites, is also present on the tip.

The path descends to Kettlewell, and lower down there are one or two springs where the lovely birdseye primrose and other wet-loving plants grow, such as the purple flowered butterwort. In her book *Pennine Flowers*, Joan Duncan says the birdseye primrose is one of the loveliest of Pennine flowering plants. It has several lilac-pink flowers on a long slender stem growing from a rosette of leaves. The top of the stem and the leaves are a floury white – hence the old name of mealy primrose. It is used on the Yorkshire Dales Society badge and is very local in its distribution. The sight of this delightful and rather special flower should brighten the day of any walker. The field path returns us to Kettlewell Bridge.

WALK 16: BUCKDEN PIKE

Start:	Buckden. Grid Ref: 942 772
Distance:	8 miles (13km)
OS Maps:	Outdoor Leisure 30 or Landranger 98
Walking Time:	4½ hours

This is a great walk, with a lovely start along the Wharfe Valley to Starbotton, to join the old route over to Wensleydale known as the Walden Road. There is a climb of 1,570 feet (480m) to the top of Buckden Pike which, at 2,302 feet (702m) above sea level, is just eight feet (2m) lower than Great Whernside. The steep descent brings you through Rakes Wood and into the car park at Buckden. There are some very boggy patches on the tops, and it may be worth waiting for a period of dry weather or a hard frost to avoid the worst. There is a large National Park car park at Buckden.

Buckden lies in a strategic position, at a junction of three ways: the road up Langstrothdale to Hawes, the road over the pass into Bishopdale and that down the Wharfe. There is also a fourth route, that of the Roman road from Buckden to Bainbridge. In later times this track was used as a drove road to bring herds of sheep and cattle to the autumn fairs at Buckden and beyond. The village itself started as a foresters' lodge within the hunting forests, and is now the last village of the dale. It has a beautiful setting and is popular with visitors, having the services of the eighteenth century Buck Inn, the village stores and a large car park. It also has a good cafe and a gallery.

Walk down to and over the bridge across the Wharfe and turn immediately left off the road along the riverside. This is part of the Dales Way. What a wonderful start to any walk is this peaceful stretch of river, where the dipper, sandpiper and grey wagtail may be seen in such attractive surroundings. The dipper flies straight and low over the river or slips under the water from a stone in search for food. The common sandpiper flicks and glides on down-curved wings, and the grey wagtail wags its long black tail and flits along the river to perch on a boulder or overhanging branch, looking more yellow than grey.

The riverbanks have been artificially supported and built up against flooding, and willow saplings have been planted to prevent further erosion. The path soon leaves the river to enter a parkland of many unusual trees. There are cherry, horse chestnut, lime, giant redwood, cedar, Scots pine, willow and variegated sycamore, and others besides. One or two of the willows are growing up in a second surge of life from the old fallen trunks.

The path enters a narrow walled lane and along the edge of badly-drained land full of rushes and fallen walls. Wheatears are to be seen along here, where they nest in holes among rocks and stones. Both sexes have the white rump, but the male has a striking grey back, a black mask and wings, and buff underparts. It will often perch on a rock or post, so you can get a close look at this small, handsome bird. They are one of the earliest of the summer visitors and take part in a dancing courtship display. The male and female face each other in a shallow hollow and the male jumps into the air with its feathers puffed out, rapidly leaping backwards and forwards, finally throwing itself down in front of its mate.

Two clear springs along here provide the habitat for water-loving plants, such as the

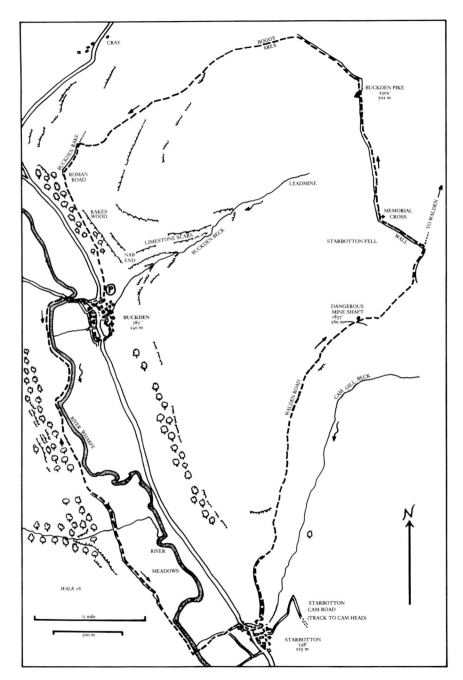

CRAY

BUCKDEN RAKE

ROMAN ROAD

RAKES WOOD

LIMESTONE SCARS

NAB END

BUCKDEN BECK

BOGGY AREA

BUCKDEN PIKE
2302'
702 m

LEADMINE

MEMORIAL CROSS

TO WALDEN

STARBOTTON FELL

WALL

P

BUCKDEN
787'
240 m

DANGEROUS MINE SHAFT
1837'
560 m

WALDEN ROAD

CAM GILL BECK

RIVER WHARFE

RIVER MEADOWS

WALK 16

½ mile

500 m

N

STARBOTTON CAM ROAD
(TRACK TO CAM HEAD)

STARBOTTON
738'
225 m

kingcup, lady's smock, watermint and various pondweeds. A deep pool contains many young fish. The kingcup or marsh marigold may be in flower as early as March, when the bright gold flowers bring welcome splashes of yellow to wet places like these. The heart-shaped leaves are green and shiny, and plants vary in size, being much smaller on high ground. Lady's smock is perhaps mostly in flower when the cuckoo is heard, and therefore is known also as cuckoo flower. It is also associated with milkmaids, another name for it. It has a delicate lilac flower and the edible leaves are a good substitute for watercress. The limestone scars which border the dale are covered in natural woodland; the trees include many yews besides the usual ash and hazel.

There are four means of crossing the river: a ford, two lots of stepping stones and chains slung from trees. Take the second lot of stepping stones, and head for the village of Starbotton along a wall built of water-worn cobbles, to join a lane which comes from the ford. There is an interesting variety of flowers along here at different seasons. Turn right through the village. Starbotton is a lovely cluster of mainly seventeenth to early nineteenth century stone houses, with a fine array of primitive upper Dales barns. The Fox and Hounds – note the case of role reversal on the sign – is a traditional Dales pub and was rebuilt in 1834 in Georgian style, since when there has been very little new building, except for one or two houses and barn conversions.

Turn left alongside the Fox and Hounds, and left again, to climb up the gravel bank to the Walden road. A short steep climb out of the valley brings fine views of the other side of the the dale. You can make out very well the different types of land from here and how it is used:

1. Poorly drained land in the valley bottom, liable to flood and full of rushes.
2. Small enclosed pastures and meadow-land on better drained lower slopes.
3. Then wooded limestone scars with mainly ash and hazel.
4. Above the scars are the higher limestone pastures, good for sheep grazing.
5. Then the rough grassland and heather of the gritstone moors.

There is a fine view down the dale from here, too.

Lady's smock.

Keep along the wall. On the right is the deep and narrow valley of Cam Gill, a rather featureless tributary of the Wharfe. However, it was in 1686 that disaster struck the village and, during a terrible storm, Cam Gill brought down torrents of water, within minutes destroying many of the newly-built cottages. Acres of good farmland were covered with the debris. To see the quiet waters of Cam Gill Beck it hardly seems possible, but a river in spate can move large boulders weighing several tons.

Pass some leadmine tips higher up, and beyond a wall there is an unguarded deep mine shaft. Take care. Keep straight on up the fell, where another track bears right. Join a wall with a gate at the far end. The Walden road goes straight on here, before turning down to Walden Head and on to West Burton and Wensleydale. Turn left through the gate. This is where the boggy patches start as you make the final slopes to the top of the ridge. This section is not a definitive right of way, but it is a traditional footpath and there should be no problem. A stile is provided near the summit.

At the ridge top a cross stands in memory of five Polish airmen who died here in a plane crash on the 31st January 1942. Besides bits of aeroplane half-buried in the concrete there is the curious bronze head of a fox. Follow the wall along the ridge, admiring the exceptionally fine views of the valley of Walden and the bulk of Great Whernside. Cross the wall to the summit. There are extensive views in the other direction too, with Pen-y-ghent and Ingleborough seen across Birks Fell.

Continue along the summit wall for a short way before following it down to the left. Then strike out through the wet ground and onto the limestone, where it is much drier underfoot. A good impression of the various Yoredale limestones is gained from the giant steps of the descent, one after the other, to Buckden Rake, which is in Great Scar limestone. There is a splendid view from here over Hubberholme into Langstrothdale. The well-built track through Rakes Wood is part of the Roman road over to Wensleydale. It is partly cut into the rock, forming a sloping terrace and built up at the outer edge. The track leads straight down to the car park.

WALK 17: BUCKDEN, CRAY, YOCKENTHWAITE AND HUBBERHOLME

Start: Buckden, National Park car park. Grid Ref: 942 772
Distance: 7 miles (11km)
OS Maps: Outdoor Leisure 30 or Landranger 98
Walking Time: 3½ hours

This walk is an old favourite, and connects Buckden with the small hamlets of Cray, Yockenthwaite and Hubberholme, incorporating a section of Roman road and a grandstand view of the valley as it traverses the head of the dale along the 1,150 foot (350m) contour. It includes a visit to the lovely Hubberholme Church, and then returns to Buckden along the river and the Dales Way. There is a large car park in Buckden.

Buckden, at the upper end of Wharfedale, lies 760 feet (235m) above sea level and is situated in a favoured spot for walkers, with a variety of beautiful scenery close by. The village began as a hunting centre on the southern edge of the forests of Langstrothdale Chase, where no doubt there were many fine bucks. Chase is another word which refers to hunting, from the French *chasse*. Hunting lodges were established higher up at Hubberholme, Deepdale, Beckermonds and Oughtershaw. Only traces now remain of the once extensive forests.

Starting from within the car park, go through the gate and along the track to Buckden Rake. This is a small surviving section of the Roman road which went from Ilkley to Bainbridge, so you can follow the legionaries' route for a short distance. The road has been cut into the rock and built up on the lower side, and is finely engineered with an even gradient through Rakes Wood. At the top, keep along the wall on the left through a gate and signed 'Cray High Bridge'. From here there is a view of Hubberholme and its attractive church. The stepped slopes of the Yoredale limestones are displayed all around. Pass through a gate with a hefty stone gatepost, then leave the Roman road and cut down to

the left to the hamlet of Cray. The collection of farm buildings which make up Cray have hardly been touched by the twentieth century, though formerly there was a larger community here.

Go round the White Lion, and follow the yellow spots through the farmyard to begin one of the most beautiful mid-level walks in the dale. Pass a barn with a narrow arched door – still used in the traditional manner – and cross over a rocky gill. The path has magnificent views down Wharfedale, looking out over the tops of the ash trees which cling to the scar below. Appearing on the left is Scar House, a substantial building and one with an interesting history. George Fox visited the original Scar House in 1652, the year when, on his travels in the north-west of England, he convinced many Seekers to become Quakers. That year is seen as the beginning of the Society of Friends. He stayed with James Tennant and his family, and James later died in York Castle for his beliefs. The present building is early Victorian and is the third one since George Fox visited it. The Quaker burial ground still exists at Scar House and was the first piece of land owned by Quakers. The walk may be shortened by descending to Hubberholme from here.

Otherwise this delightful gallery walk

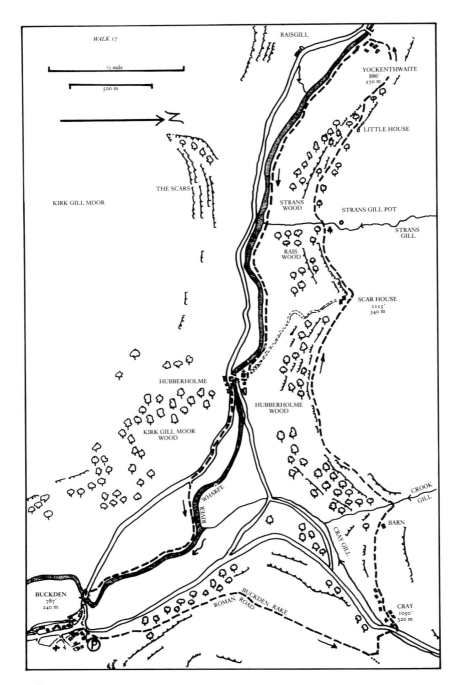

WALK 17

½ mile

500 m

N

RAISGILL

YOCKENTHWAITE
886'
270 m

LITTLE HOUSE

KIRK GILL MOOR

THE SCARS

STRANS
WOOD

STRANS GILL POT

STRANS
GILL

RAIS
WOOD

SCAR HOUSE
1115'
340 m

HUBBERHOLME

HUBBERHOLME
WOOD

KIRK GILL MOOR
WOOD

RIVER WHARFE

CROOK
GILL

BARN

CRAY GILL

BUCKDEN
787'
240 m

ROMAN ROAD

BUCKDEN RAKE

CRAY
1050'
320 m

106

continues past limestone pavements, through a small wood of pines and sycamores, across a little stone bridge over a miniature gorge, by several tumbled-down walls and barns, to where many hawthorns grow and the path descends to a lower level and to Yockenthwaite. In the wooded scars there are several woodland plants which persist in spite of sheep grazing, including yellow pimpernel, wood cranesbill and early purple orchid. Yellow pimpernel blooms from May until early autumn, its trailing stems sending up a single yellow flower of five petals on each slender stalk. Wood cranesbill, a flower of early summer, has bright purple flowers with a white centre, in contrast to meadow cranesbill with larger bluer flowers which adorn roadsides in July.

Turn down the left bank of the young River Wharfe, which dries up completely in summer when any water seeps through the limestone and runs underground. The narrow old stone bridge that spans the river in a graceful arch has survived road-building and bridge-widening, as it just serves the two farmhouses of Yocken-thwaite. Together they make a picturesque scene for any painter or photographer. The name is Irish-Norse and means 'Eogan's clearing'. Birds along the riverside include wheatear, meadow pipit, chaffinch, pied and grey wagtail. The wheatear is not usually far from rocks or old walls, where it finds a hole to nest. Its food consists mainly of insects and larvae, and sometimes it can be seen hovering near the ground to dive on its prey, but usually it chases insects on the ground as it hops and flutters along.

The path follows the Dales Way below Strans Wood and Rais Wood, remnants of ancient woodland which hang on the limestone scars, mainly ash trees mixed with hawthorn and hazel. Wooded scars like these are characteristic of Wharfedale and carry with them a rich variety of plant life.

Further on, the river has cut into some glacial deposits, and the valley narrows as a result. Glacially-scratched limestone pebbles in the boulder clay are proof of the movement and grinding action of a former glacier. It shouldn't be too difficult to find one of these scratched pebbles.

Quite suddenly you come upon Hubberholme Church, dedicated to St Michael and All Angels. This old church is the most attractive in the dale, yet it has a solidness and dignity about it, with its sturdy tower and broad low roof, that invite further inspection. Here is a lovely building, dating mainly from the twelfth century and constructed of local stone on a perfect site by the Skirfare which is totally in keeping with its surroundings. Pass through the old studded door and examine the very fine oak rood loft erected in 1558. It is painted red, black and gold and although there are some bits missing it adds, together with the iron candelabra and low arches, to the ancient atmosphere of the interior. Stained glass records local history, and the fine oak pews were made in the 1930s by Robert Thompson of Kilburn. You will see his trademark of a carved mouse. (His work can also to be seen in York Minster.) Hubberholme was a favourite haunt of the grand old man of English literature, J B Priestley, who wrote that it was one of the pleasantest places in the world and whose ashes are buried in the churchyard.

Over the bridge is the George Inn, once the vicarage of Hubberholme. On the first Monday of the New Year it is still the scene of a candle auction for the lease of sixteen acres (6ha) of grazing land, a tradition of 200 years which raises money for the poor of the parish. A candle is lit and the proceedings must be over before it burns out. A festive time is had by all, and it is only during the last few minutes in the life of the candle that serious bids are made. The

Hubberholme and Langstrothdale.

bridge appears to be almost identical to that in Threshfield, with huge dressed top-stones along the parapet. For a time this bridge was on the main highway from Lancaster to Newcastle-upon-Tyne. The

previous one was washed away about 1748.

The Dales Way takes to the road for the next few hundred yards, bordered by sweet cicely, butterbur, silverweed and dog's mercury. Sweet cicely is common all up the

Wood cranesbill (bottom) and meadow cranesbill.

before the leaves, which are large and were once were used to wrap up butter. Silverweed is related to tormentil, but it is one of the few British wild flowers to have silvery grey leaves. Its creeping stems and yellow flowers are often found along the edge of the road.

Turn off to walk along the riverside, with more butterbur growing near the water and the addition of planted willows to reinforce the banks. Some of the older trees have had their roots washed out of the soil, and are now standing half in the water. The bridge in Buckden was built to replace the bridge which was washed away in about 1748 in Hubberholme. It became known as the 'election bridge', when a prospective Member of Parliament promised a new bridge to the people of Buckden if they voted for him.

The bridge is a good place to observe dipper, sandpiper, and pied and grey wagtails. A few paces further returns you to the centre of Buckden.

dale. The leaves and seeds smell strongly of aniseed, and the foliage and roots have been used as a vegetable.

The pink flowery spikes of butterbur come through the ground early in the spring,

WALK 18: THE MONK'S ROAD AND HAWKSWICK COTE

Start: Arncliffe. Grid Ref: 931 718
Distance: 10 miles (16km)
OS Maps: Outdoor Leisure 10 or Landranger 98
Walking Time: 5 hours

This is a full day's outing. You should be completely self-contained, as it can be exposed with little shelter, and there are no shops or pubs on the way. The walk follows two ancient monastic routes, the Monk's Road from Arncliffe to Malham, and a similar one from Malham to Hawkswick. Both are well-built footpaths, easy to follow and enclose the largest Site of Special Scientific Interest in Wharfedale. There is limited parking space round the village green.

Arncliffe is a lovely village. Its limestone farmhouses and cottages overlook the large village green, bordered by tall sycamores. One of them is a house-turned-barn with a datestone which reads 'TFA 1667', and at the far corner of the green is the Falcon, a favourite pub in the dale. In a beautiful position by the River Skirfare stands the attractive church, with its early tower and tasteful nineteenth century restoration. Inside is a display of church silver, a list of the names of the Littondale men who fought at Flodden in 1513 and a pike which one of them may have carried. Near the other bridge at the top of the village, under which flows Cowside Beck, is a noted site for an unusual flower. It grows five feet (1½ m) tall and goes by the name of saracens woundwort (*Senecio fluviatalis*), a species of ragwort which flowers in late summer. The bridge, incidentally, carries a warning that it is not constructed to take traction engines or steam wagons!

Start off along the walled lane to the right of the Falcon, signed Malham, and pass a Georgian house converted from Arncliffe Mill, which once spun yarn for cottage weavers in nearby villages. In summer the lane is lined with yellow monkey flower, blue meadow cranesbill and good King Henry. This last plant has greenish-yellow flowers, grows to twenty inches (50 cm) tall

and was eaten as a vegetable in medieval times – a sort of fifteenth century cabbage.

Turn off the green lane before it steepens at the sign to Malham, and strike up the hillside to the Monk's Road and the first of seven ladder stiles. The limestone pasture is full of small flowers in the summer: wild thyme and fairy flax are common, the latter looking like a miniature stitchwort. Rockrose and birdseye primrose also grow along the path.

From here are fine views up the scenic valley of Littondale, with its many stone walls and scattered barns, and also back to Arncliffe in its picturesque setting where Cowside Beck enters the Skirfare. Littondale is the most perfect and beautiful of the Dales. Its straight, flat-bottomed, steep-sided appearance give it the textbook glacial shape. In only eight miles (12km) nestle the small communities of Hawkswick, Arncliffe, Litton, Halton Gill and Foxup, and interrupting the symmetry of the dale are the many narrow side gills, in which flow becks with names such as Cosh, Potts, Crystal, Cowside and Cote.

As you gain height you get a good view of the V-shaped valley of Cowside Beck – a quiet, winding, water-eroded valley, in contrast to Littondale. Cowside is noted for its many wild flowers – it is said that once the rare and beautiful lady's slipper orchid

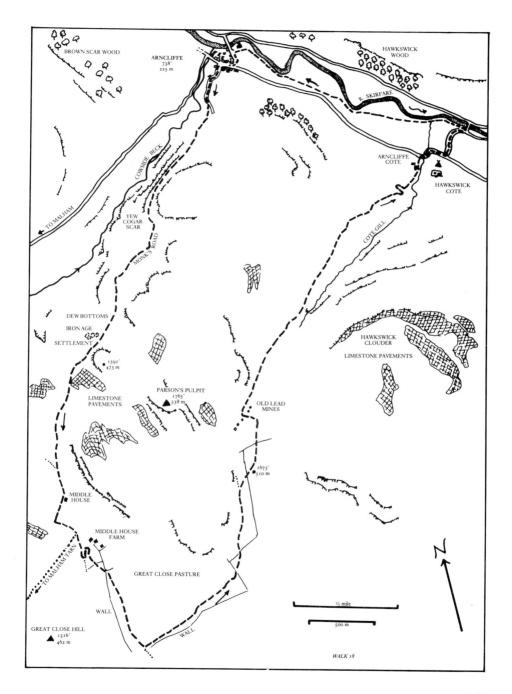

BROWN SCAR WOOD

ARNCLIFFE
738'
225 m

HAWKSWICK
WOOD

R. SKIRFARE

COWSIDE BECK

ARNCLIFFE
COTE

HAWKSWICK
COTE

TO MALHAM

YEW
COGAR
SCAR

MONK'S ROAD

COTE GILL

DEW BOTTOMS

IRON AGE
SETTLEMENT

HAWKSWICK
CLOUDER

LIMESTONE PAVEMENTS

1591'
475 m

LIMESTONE
PAVEMENTS

PARSON'S PULPIT
1765'
538 m

OLD LEAD
MINES

1673'
510 m

MIDDLE
HOUSE

MIDDLE HOUSE
FARM

TO MALHAM TARN

GREAT CLOSE PASTURE

½ mile

500 m

WALL

GREAT CLOSE HILL
1516'
462 m

WALL

N

WALK 18

grew here, but all the plants were plundered and reappeared for a short time in local gardens. The path continues along a terrace high above the unseen Yew Cogar Scar, crosses a ravine and joins scars on the left with benches of limestone jutting out to the right.

On one of these is Dew Bottoms, the site of an Iron Age family farm. Some of the soil has been eroded away, leaving bare limestone pavement, and the low stone and turf banks are the remains of stockaded field boundaries. There are five small fields, four hut circles and two rectangular ones, with a wide area of pasture all around. Arthur Raistrick suggested the central circular mound was a large round hut that belonged to the head of the family group, and that his sons and others were housed in the three smaller huts. This is one of the best of the early Iron Age settlements and may have been in use in the Bronze Age. It is a good place to look for flints dug up by moles and rabbits. If you find any, do label them as later you may wish to donate them to a local museum.

Continue across a broad, rough, grassy area with a spring-fed dewpond, until an impressive limestone scar comes into view on the left and trees in the distance denote the renovated Middle House. Before this farm was built there was a Cistercian grange here, a clue to which may be seen in the close, irregular pattern of stone walls. The enclosed fields are very small and variable, and of an early date, contrasting with the large rectangular fields further away, which are eighteenth century.

Beyond this isolated farmhouse is a striking new view over Malhamdale, although strangely enough Malham Tarn is hidden. The path skirts an area known as High Midge Hills to a ladder stile overlooking the big working farm of Middle House Farm, a building which looks more like Lakeland architecture than that of the Yorkshire Dales. Go through the wooden stile in the fence, and cross the farm track and the gate at the end of the wall. This leads onto East Great Close, a very large pasture. It was on Great Close that the biggest of all the cattle markets used to take place. Four or five thousand cattle were gathered here to be bought and sold, having been driven south from Scotland in the days before the railways. They came along a high route along the side of the Eden Valley, including Lady Anne Clifford's Way in Mallerstangdale, avoiding villages and cropland, and serving other markets on the way.

Keep within 100 yards (90 m) of the wall which is on the right. The upper part of Goredale Beck can be seen straight ahead, though Malham Tarn is now hidden by Great Close Hill. Near the far end of this pasture, turn left along tractor tracks, still with a wall on the right, and up the hill to a gate. The path here has joined another ancient monastic route from Malham to Hawkswick and Kettlewell. Like the Monk's Road, it passes through exhilarating limestone scenery to descend alongside Cote Gill into Littondale again. From the gate there are long-distance views into Lancashire, with Pendle Hill's characteristic whaleback shape sixteen miles (25km) away, but Malham Tarn is still elusive.

Ahead, new scars come into view and the path turns northward as it rises to 1,650 feet (500m) above sea level. A fingerpost indicates Parson's Pulpit and Arncliffe Cote. Taking the latter route, pass through a small gate – too small for a modern tractor but big enough for a packhorse – and in the broken-down wall look for fossil crinoids and brachiopods, the sea-lilies and lamp shells in this Yoredale lagoonal limestone. Look out also for the peregrine. Our route encloses a large area of high wild limestone country, and it is worth keeping an eye on

Oystercatcher.

the sky to catch a glimpse of this beautiful bird soaring on level wings high above its hunting grounds. Once it has spotted its prey, such as a rabbit, it stoops in a headlong dive with wings close together, reaching speeds of 95 to 155 mph (150 to 250 kph). Peregrine populations have recovered well in recent years and there is a fair chance of seeing one in the wilder parts of the dale.

Another small gate passes through a substantial wall with an enormous rock incorporated into it, and which forms a parish boundary. Buckden Pike and Great Whernside stand out ahead, and the path then winds downhill past old pits to a lead vein on the right, and a limekiln in a very good state of preservation on the left. The red rocks in the kiln are an indication of the heat attained in the burning process.

Cote Gill, Littondale.

Walk a few yards over to the right for a glance at a pretty waterfall at the head of Cote Gill. There is also a spectacular view down the gill, as the rock layers can be followed round Hawkswick Clouder where scree and bare limestone adorn the fellside. Flowers typical of limestone pastures grow here, and include the lemon-coloured mouse-eared hawkweed, rockrose, wild thyme and milkwort.

The path follows tractor tracks to a gate in the wall, away from the gill, to descend to Arncliffe Cote. Turn right at the road, round the corner, then left to the foot-bridge. Opposite the turn-off there is a totally overgrown 'green lane' to a barn full of inpenetrable blackthorn. At the foot-bridge, follow the path to Arncliffe up-stream along the left side of the River Skirfare.

This is a good locality to see the oyster-catcher, another bird which has increased its population in recent years. This increase is because it has found new inland breeding habitats, such as this area of Littondale where it nests on the riverside shingle. The shrill 'kleep-kleep' soon draws your attention to two or three of these waders as they fly low over the river. Their bold black and white plumage and long orange bills are also very conspicuous. The nest is a mere hollow among the pebbles, and you may see the birds probing for worms and insects in the riverside fields.

In summer they are joined by common sandpiper, redshank, three kinds of wagtail and dozens of sand martins. The yellow wagtail is a summer visitor and its brilliant yellow plumage make it unmistakable. It has a harsh call note of 'tswee-ip', often heard in May when it can be seen perching on a wire fence or bush. A bridge over a side stream brings you close to the river again, where there is a remarkable vertical bank of river gravels some twelve feet (4m) high, where the sand martins find thin layers of sand for their nesting holes. The path returns past St Oswald's Church into the village of Arncliffe.

WALK 19: PEN-Y-GHENT FROM LITTON

Start: Litton. Grid Ref: 905 741
Distance: 14 miles (22½ km)
OS Maps: Outdoor Leisure 30 or Landranger 98
Walking Time: 7 hours

This is the big one. Along the valley first to Foxup, then, skirting the northern slopes of this distinctive mountain, the route strikes steeply up onto Plover Hill and along the ridge to the summit of Pen-y-ghent itself. It follows the Pennine Way on the descent to Rainscar, and picks up one of the finest tracks in the dale, across Dawson Close and back to Litton. Be prepared for a long day, mixed weather and some rough and steep paths. There is space for only a few cars in Litton.

The quiet little village of Litton is a small collection of mostly eighteenth century houses, with a post office, a pub – the Queen's Arms – but no church or chapel. Of two of its houses, one used to be an inn and the other a school, as the village was a busier place at one time. A circular hollow on the lower side of the village was once the cockpit where the eighteenth century murderer Tom Lee brought his fighting cock. When his bird lost, it was said he would not accept the verdict or pay his bets, so was ducked in the river and driven out of town. Water supplies are almost all from spring water, and a large and powerful spring can be seen flowing out of the valley side across the dale. The name Litton means 'village on a torrent'.

Pen-y-ghent is the lowest of the Three Peaks and at 2,277 feet (694m) is a little lower than Great Whernside and Buckden Pike. However, as my grandfather used to say: 'Pendle, Pen-y-ghent, Whernside and Ingleborough, you'll ne'er find such hills if you search England thorough!' These are the mountains that stand out, each one isolated and each with its own easily recognisable profile, and it is these that have the fame and the glory.

Turn left at the far end of the green to the bridge over the river. In the summer the poor River Skirfare is not always there,

often just a few pools of water and bare stretches of limestone. Half the time it flows unseen underground, which must be rather confusing for the fish and other inhabitants which like to have the water moving around them! Cross the fields to Spittle Croft, now barns but once a long-house and once the site of a monks' resting place belonging to Fountains Abbey. There is a story that there is buried treasure left by a farmer who lived here and minted coins in an underground room.

Turn right into a green lane and, at the stone bridge, ignore the track up the hill to the left, which is the return route. Keep near the river, following a wall and gate along the path to Nether Hesleden. A barn by the path has a circular window. In summer there are wheatears, oystercatchers and curlews about. You will no doubt see and hear several curlews on this walk at any time from February to October. What a wonderful, ringing call the curlew has and a thrilling song of slow, then accelerating liquid notes and bubbling trill; and what an elegant, almost aristocratic bird this is. No diving and flapping about like the lapwing, but a straight and powerful flight and a long glide, bill lowered, concorde-like, as it makes a landing.

Pen-y-ghent comes into view for the first time, and Pen-y-ghent Gill is crossed by

Pen-y-ghent from the improved Pennine Way footpath.

the bridge at Nether Hesleden Farm. Go straight on past the large green storage tank and through the fields to Foxup. There are several fine barns along here, which display some interesting features. One has had living accommodation at one end for the farm hand. The roofs of one or two barns have been repaired with purple Welsh and green Cumbrian slate, though most still have a Yorkshire flagstone roof. Join the river again just before Halton Gill Bridge and follow it to Foxup. Here Cosh Beck and Foxup Beck come together to make the beginnings of the River Skirfare. This is the end of the road up Littondale and here is a small farming community, the farm-houses overlooking the beck, two or three of them having their own stone bridge to the front door.

At Foxup turn left up the lane to the second little stone bridge, then left up the hillside, following the sign for Horton-in-Ribblesdale, to a gate on the right. This is a bridleway marked with blue-topped posts. In fact it is known as Foxup Road, another old monastic route over to Horton, which climbs onto the side of Plover Hill, making use of a shelf of limestone. From this level you can see Ingleborough and Whernside, the latter being the higher at 2,419 feet (736m) and the highest of the Three Peaks. The old road traverses Foxup Moor, but our path leaves it to turn left straight up the mountainside at the sign 'Penyghent 2', scaling a gritstone scar and up onto the top of Plover Hill. From the scar there is a fine view, and one can pick out the route which continues to Horton. The ridge from

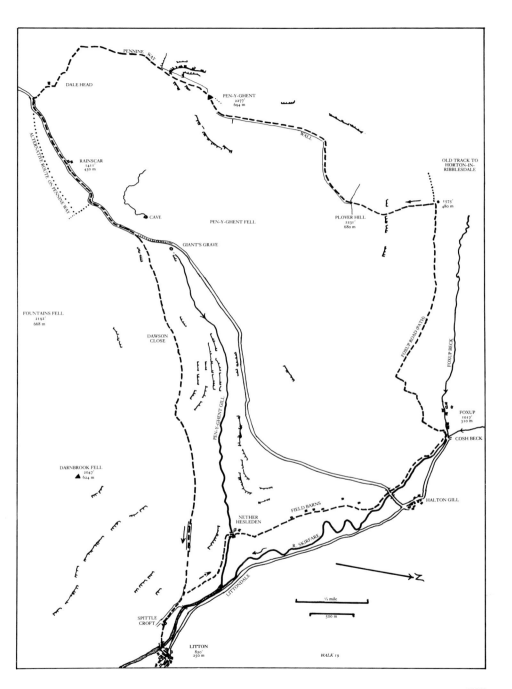

PENNINE WAY

DALE HEAD

PEN-Y-GHENT
2277'
694 m

ALTERNATIVE ROUTE ON PENNINE WAY

RAINSCAR
1411'
430 m

CAVE

PEN-Y-GHENT FELL

GIANT'S GRAVE

WALL

OLD TRACK TO
HORTON-IN-
RIBBLESDALE

1575'
480 m

PLOVER HILL
2231'
680 m

FOUNTAINS FELL
2192'
668 m

DAWSON
CLOSE

PEN-Y-GHENT GILL

FOXUP ROAD (PATH)

FOXUP BECK

FOXUP
1017'
310 m

COSH BECK

DARNBROOK FELL
2047'
624 m

FIELD BARNS

NETHER
HESLEDEN

HALTON GILL

R. SKIRFARE

LITTONDALE

½ mile

500 m

SPITTLE
CROFT

LITTON
820'
250 m

WALK 19

Plover Hill to Pen-y-ghent forms the main watershed of England. Drainage on the west side of the mountain goes into the Ribble, which flows into the Irish Sea, and the waters of Pen-y-ghent Gill on the other side flow eventually into the North Sea.

From Plover Hill, follow the wall and a rather boggy route eventually to cross the wall to the summit of Pen-y-ghent. In summer, hare's tail cotton grass flowers here, the single cottony fruit-heads bobbing in the breeze. It is in this area you are most likely to see a raven. This is the largest of the crow family and is a good six inches (15cm) longer than the carrion crow, from which it can be distinguished by its more powerful and slower wing beats, and noisy, deep-throated 'prruk prruk'. Watch it as it glides and soars, sometimes tumbling or diving in acrobatic display flight. Plover Hill is well named, as you will probably hear the sorrowful call of the golden plover up here between March and September.

The top of Pen-y-ghent is grassy, with an all-round panoramic view. Mountains of the southern Lake District, Ribblesdale, Ingleborough and Whernside, Morecambe Bay, Pendle Hill and Fountains Fell all contribute to make one of the finest views in the Pennines. In the mid-1700s, Miles Wilson, a parson from Halton Gill, wrote a story called *The Man on the Moon* in which a local cobbler put a ladder on the top of Pen-y-ghent to reach the moon. The man soon came down again as he didn't like the food.

Continue in the same southerly direction to descend steeply over a gritstone edge, followed by a limestone scar. In April look on the white limestone cliffs for splashes of magenta of the beautiful purple saxifrage, where cushions of it adorn the rocks. Binoculars can be useful here. The purple or mountain saxifrage is a survivor of an arctic-alpine flora which grew in Britain soon after the Ice Age. With later growth of woodland, many such species were squeezed out, though some, like the purple saxifrage, survived on rocky cliffs at high altitude, where we see it today.

From the summit the path – part of the Pennine Way – is very steep and gets heavy use. Improvements have been made lower down to restrict erosion. As a result, walking is made easier by the use of raised boarded walks, special matting and a more permanent structure is finished in a cover of limestone chippings. The pothole of Milk Churn Hole is at a crossing of the ways, but follow the sign to Dale Head and the road.

Although a further section of the Pennine Way can be used, it is more pleasant along the road. So turn left, passing Rainscar Farm before taking the right fork on the track to Litton. For those with the time and interest, there is the Giant's Grave, the remains of an ancient multiple tomb or passage grave, 400 yards (365m) further along the road. It was built by the Neolithic (or New Stone Age) people who lived between 4000 and 2000 BC. However, the remains are scanty and disappointing.

The track to Litton is a splendid walk with fine views, again an old monks' way and packhorse route, this one between Stainforth in Ribblesdale and Litton, with a continuation over to Buckden and on into Wensleydale. In spring and autumn you may see large flocks of fieldfares and redwings in this area, and look out for the more secretive snipe.

Near the beginning of this monks' route there is a limestone scar on the right which contains fossil corals. If you have failed to find any on the track, a small waterfall on the right, on a stretch of fell called Dawson Close, will reveal a small coral reef. The corals are a colonial type with the broad name of *Lithostrotion* and are quite common

Snipe.

in the limestones of the Dales. In cross-section the coral appears as small wheels with spokes and, when weathered, as slender tubes.

Continue along the track past two field kilns on the right and a seven foot (2m) tall Silurian slate gatepost with a bench mark on it. Wonderful views up and down Lit-tondale reveal themselves as the track starts to descend. Soon you rejoin the Skirfare at New Bridge, returning to Litton along the green lane to Spittle Croft and through the fields to the village. Alternatively, if it is quiet, you may like to finish by walking along the road, from which there is a good view of the river and its birdlife.

WALK 20: HALTON GILL, HORSE HEAD MOOR AND BECKERMONDS

Start: Halton Gill. Grid Ref: 880 765
Distance: 8 miles (13km)
OS Maps: Outdoor Leisure 30 or Landranger 98
Walking Time: 4 hours

Here is an energetic walk with a climb of nearly 1,000 feet (300m) to the top of Horse Head Moor and the reward of an extensive panoramic view, a visit to Langstrothdale and the Yockenthwaite stone circle. You can see the beginning of the River Wharfe at Beckermonds where the two becks meet. The return is over the top once again, through the landslip scenery overlooking Foxup and the narrowing upper end of Littondale. There is limited parking space in Halton Gill.

The small, attractive hamlet of Halton Gill nestles serenely at the foot of Horse Head Moor at the far end of Littondale. It is a fascinating little place. For four centuries this community had its own church and by 1626 a small grammar school, founded by two brothers, Henry and William Fawcett. The brothers grew up here and made their money from the wool trade in Norwich. The school, schoolmaster's cottage and chapel were all in the same small building, which is now a private house close to the road. The lintel over the door where the schoolmaster lived reads '1626 WF' (William Fawcett). There is a fine collection of farmhouses, cottages and barns, and the various dated lintels show them to be older than those of Litton, being mainly seventeenth century. The beautiful old hall with its mullioned windows is dated 1641.

Surrounded by good permanent pastures on the lower slopes and further limited grazing on the fells, sheep farming is the main occupation. At sheep shearing time or when dipped in the autumn, sheep are still 'scored' or counted in twenties, though the old Dales method of rhythmic counting is no longer used. It is a system which may be of Celtic origin: *yan, tan tethera, fethera, pits*; there are many written

variations, one of which continues: *tayter, layter, overa, covera, disk*. The hand knitters used the same way of counting stitches.

Although today Halton Gill appears rather isolated, formerly it was on a crossroads of packhorse routes and became an important stopping point for packhorse trains *en route* between Ribblesdale and Wensleydale. For six centuries packhorses were the main form of transport. They were still used in the leadmining districts until Victorian times, where terrain was difficult. Horses and ponies carried over 2cwt (100kg) of goods balanced in two panniers or baskets; they took all kinds of loads such as coal, salt, charcoal, corn and wool. Between twenty and forty animals made up a train, with a driver and one or two attendants in charge.

The walk follows one of these packhorse routes over to Yockenthwaite, and begins by going up through the village and off to the right up a cart track signed 'Hawes'. Even a short climb gives you a good view of Foxup and, doubling back, you have a magnificent view down Littondale over the rooftops of Halton Gill below. Keep to the wide track, a well-engineered road with an even gradient, making the climb easy. In fact this track is the only section of the old road from Settle to Hawes that has not

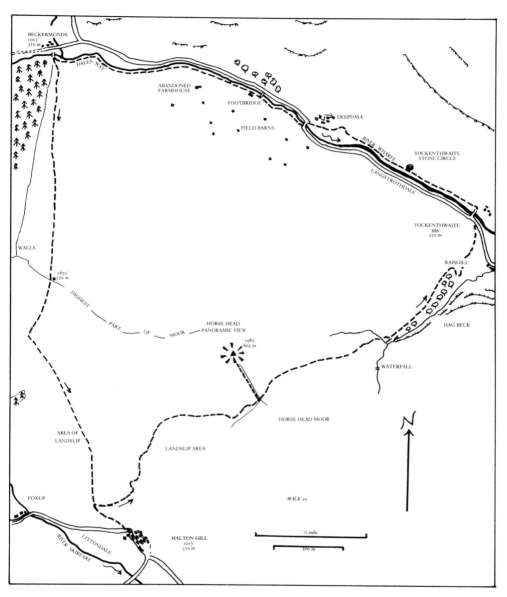

been surfaced. The hummocky nature of the valley side across Halton Gill Beck indicates landslipping in the Yoredales on this steep slope. As you get higher, the peaks of Ingleborough and Pen-y-ghent come into view to the rear, and you cross Halton Gill Beck and its branching streamlets.

Continue to the top of Horse Head Pass and turn left along the wall to the trig point at 1,985 feet (605m) on the summit of Horse Head. (The short distance from the bridleway to this stunning viewpoint is not a right of way.) On a clear day this is one of the best views in the dale. It is a truly panoramic 360 degree viewpoint, with the Langdale Pikes in the southern Lake District, Wild Boar Fell and Mallerstang Edge, Great Shunner Fell and Addlebrough, Buckden Pike and Great Whernside, Old Cote Moor, Fountains Fell, Pen-y-ghent, Ingleborough and Whernside all visible on a clear day. Only the view from the top of Pen-y-ghent can beat this one.

Go back to Horse Head Gate, the top of the pass for the descent into Langstrothdale. Much of the route from now on is in newly-acquired National Trust land. Again there are fine views, this time into part of the valley of the upper Wharfe as you look across to Yockenthwaite Moor. Fossil corals occur in the path where a little stream crosses it and flows down into Hagg Beck. To see the waterfalls, descend a few

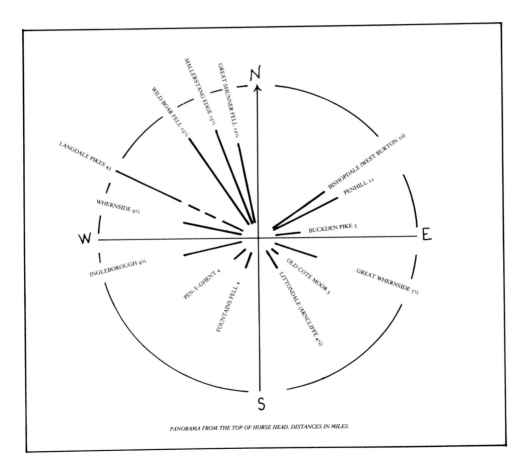

PANORAMA FROM THE TOP OF HORSE HEAD. DISTANCES IN MILES.

paces into the gill and turn upstream. At the foot of the deep gorge, carved by Hagg beck, is Raisgill, a single farmhouse which like Yockenthwaite, Kirk Gill and Cray, was originally an isolated Norse settlement.

Cross the beautifully-shaped single span bridge at Yockenthwaite where it crosses the Wharfe, and turn up the dale for a delightful riverside walk. A couple of fields along is the Yockenthwaite stone circle of the Bronze Age (1,800 to 2,000 BC) the best in Wharfedale. It measures only twenty-five feet (7m) across and contains some twenty stones almost touching each other. There is a hint of an outer row of stones to the north-west and, since none of them are very large, it is possible some of the outer ones have been taken for use in wall-building. It seems an odd site for a stone circle, which are often situated in high, prominent places, and it has been suggested this may be a place of burial. (Another stone circle in Upper Wharfedale is at Fancarl Top, off the B6265 near Grimwith Reservoir.)

The Bronze Age Yockenthwaite stone circle.

Yockenthwaite.

Continue to Deepdale, and cross the iron bridge to the other bank of the river where it is constricted to a narrow strid near an old farmhouse. In the adjoining fields there are as many as ten barns and the rather fine ruin of Cowside House. These reflect the former wealth and fertility of the surrounding hillside, the soils here being of deep, glacial origin in contrast to the usual thin soil that develops on limestone. Look out along this beautiful stretch of river for the grey wagtail and kingfisher. With

disturbance along both banks of the river by walkers on the Dales Way and picnickers along the road, birds such as the grey wagtail may be driven from the area but at the moment seem to be hanging on. Whereas pied and yellow wagtails do nest and thrive away from rivers, for the grey wagtail the river is its true habitat.

Here the young Wharfe flows along limestone bedrock, with attractive miniature waterfalls, pools and rapids. It is a beautiful stretch and soon you reach Beckermonds – Norse for 'the meeting of the becks' – where the River Wharfe has its beginning. Its source streams are Green Field Beck and Oughtershaw Beck, which meet here for everyone to see in front of the neat houses which make up Beckermonds. It is possible to explore these two tributary valleys on foot, and both of them lead into the upper part of Ribblesdale. At Cam Houses the Dales Way joins and crosses the Pennine Way.

Turn up alongside the plantation where the sign is to Halton Gill. At an altitude of 1,150 to 1,650 feet (350-500m) these conifers are in a fairly exposed position, but despite this they are growing well, though still open enough to support a variety of wildlife. It is in this sort of habitat that the sparrowhawk likes to hunt. This fast-flying bird of prey will dash in and out of the trees quite near the ground. It may perch on a fence post before making another attacking foray in amongst the firs, as it searches for an unsuspecting chaffinch, starling or meadow pipit.

A glance back from the hillside gives a fine view of the two valleys of Oughtershaw and Green Field, one behind the other, with limestone pavements and forest plantations. The path gradually veers away from the wall and, if you lose the path, the wall is a good guide. Exactly one mile from Beckermonds is the top of the ridge and a ladder stile. Soon you begin to descend, and there is a bird's-eye view of Cosh and Foxup at the very end of Littondale. Cosh Beck and Foxup Beck eventually run together at Foxup Bridge to form the Skirfare. A left turn is indicated along the contour and over the wall into Great Pasture, and more landslip scenery. It is the textbook situation of thick, strong Yoredale limestones on top of soft shales. The shales became lubricated by groundwater and gave way, so that a whole section of hillside has sagged and slipped to produce this extraordinary hummocky landscape. The slip probably happened during a warm and wet climatic period about 6,000 years ago, long after the ice had melted from the valley.

The path descends rapidly, joins the Horse Head track and returns to Halton Gill.

SELECTED READING

Arthur Raistrick, *The Pennine Dales* (Eyre and Spottiswoode, 1968). A broad look at the Yorkshire Dales, the geology, pre-history and historical development.

Tony Waltham, *Yorkshire Dales National Park* (Webb and Bower, 1987). The latest official guide to the National Park. Well-written and informative.

Geoffrey N Wright, *The Yorkshire Dales* (David and Charles, 1986). Informative on natural history, history, mining and quarrying. Includes a gazetteer.

Geology:

Arthur Raistrick and John L Illingworth, *The Face of North West Yorkshire* (Dalesman, 1959). A background to geology and natural vegetation.

Tony Waltham, *Yorkshire Dales: Limestone Country* (Constable, 1987). A useful guide to limestone caves, crags and gorges.

W Edwards and F M Trotter, *The Pennines and Adjacent Areas* (HMSO). Geological Survey regional handbook of the area.

History:

Peter Gunn, *The Yorkshire Dales. Landscape with Figures* (Century Publishing, 1984). Brings the Dales history to life.

Harry Speight, *Upper Wharfedale* (Elliot Stock, 1900. Reprint by Smith Settle, 1988). A reliable and scholarly history.

Ella Pontefract and Marie Hartley, *Wharfedale* (Dent, 1938. Reprint by Smith Settle, 1988). Full of readable and interesting information about the dale.

Arthur Raistrick, *Old Yorkshire Dales* (David and Charles, 1967). Much about Wharfedale, including the yeoman farmer's house in Conistone.

R W Morris, *Yorkshire through Place Names* (David and Charles, 1982). Relates settlement and place names to the geography and geology.

Geoffrey N Wright, *Roads and Trackways of the Yorkshire Dales* (Moorland Publishing, 1985). A new and attractive study of a little recorded subject.

James Walton, *Homesteads of the Yorkshire Dales* (1947. Dalesman, 1979). A short guide to Dales architecture.

Arthur Raistrick, *Buildings of the Yorkshire Dales* (Dalesman, 1976). The buildings and who built them, when and how.

Barbara Hutton and Joyce Martin. *Doorways in the Dales* (North Yorkshire and Cleveland Vernacular Buildings Study Group, 1986). A fine collection of dated door lintels with drawings and notes.

Elizabeth Raistrick, *Village Schools, an Upper Wharfedale History* (Dalesman, 1971). Some fascinating local history.

Arthur Raistrick, *Pennine Walls* (Dalesman, 1988). Who built them, why and how.

Peter Watkins, *Bolton Priory and its Church* (Church of St Mary and St Cuthbert, Bolton Abbey, 1989). A well-researched book full of interesting information.

Arthur Raistrick, *Monks and Shepherds in the Yorkshire Dales* (YDNP 1980). Activities of the monks of Fountains Abbey and Bolton Priory.

Susan D Brooks, *Parish and People of the Yorkshire Dales through ten Centuries* (Published by the author, 1973). The Church and its effect on local life.

J M Dickinson, *Mines and t'Miners, a History of Leadmining in Airedale, Wharfedale and Nidderdale* (Published by the author, 1972). Good section on Wharfedale.

Arthur Raistrick, *Lead mining in the Mid-Pennines* (D Bradford Barton, 1973). Much on leadmining in Wharfedale.

R Geoffrey Rowley, *Tom Lee, the Grassington Murderer* (The Craven Herald, 1982). Just about everything that is known about this infamous character.

Colin Speakman, *Legends of the Yorkshire Dales* (North Yorkshire Marketing, 1990). A modern interpretation of some of the old folk tales.

Natural History:

W R Mitchell and R W Robson, *Pennine Birds* (Dalesman, 1973). Useful for birds of the uplands.

J Ferguson-Lees (and others), *The Shell Guide to the Birds of Britain and Ireland* (Michael Joseph, 1983). A very good general bird book.

Sylvia Arnold, *Wild Flowers of the Yorkshire Dales* (Hutton Press, 1988). Of local interest with a chapter on each dale.

Joan E Duncan and R W Robson, *Pennine Flowers* (Dalesman, 1977). Flowers of the uplands with a section on plant lore.

Franklyn Perring, *RSNC Guide to British Wild Flowers* (Country Life Books, 1984). Very useful for learning common species and sorting out 'look-alikes'.

S L Sutton and H E Beaumont, *Butterflies and Moths of Yorkshire* (Yorkshire Naturalists Union, 1989). The first ever Yorkshire lepidoptera, 380 pages packed with information of 1,591 recorded species.

M J Delany (ed), *Yorkshire Mammals* (University of Bradford, 1985). Detailed description of species with useful distribution maps.

Walking:

Colin Speakman, *The Dales Way* (Dalesman, 1970). Over half of it deals with Wharfedale.

Colin Speakman, *Walking in the Yorkshire Dales* (Hale, 1982). A comprehensive and authoritative guide.

Arthur Gemmell and Colin Speakman, *Dales Way Route Guide, with Associated Walks* (Stile Publications, 4th ed 1988). Very good maps and return routes.

INDEX

Illustrations are numbered in italics